The Best of All Possible Worlds

More by David Arnason

The Best of All Possible Worlds

Reflections on the Interlake

David Arnason

TURNSTONE PRESS

The Best of All Possible Worlds
copyright © David Arnason

Turnstone Press
Artspace Building
206-100 Arthur Street
Winnipeg, MB
R3B 1H3 Canada
www.TurnstonePress.com

Turnstone Press gratefully acknowledges the assistance of the Canada Council for the Arts, the Manitoba Arts Council, the Government of Canada, and the Province of Manitoba through the Book Publishing Tax Credit and the Book Publisher Marketing Assistance Program.

Printed and bound in Canada by Friesens for Turnstone Press.

Library and Archives Canada Cataloguing in Publication

Arnason, David, 1940-, author
      The best of all possible worlds : reflections on the interlake / David Arnason

Issued in print and electronic formats.
ISBN 978-0-88801-625-6 (softcover).--ISBN 978-0-88801-626-3 (EPUB).--
ISBN 978-0-88801-627-0 (Kindle).--ISBN 978-0-88801-628-7 (PDF)

      1. Arnason, David, 1940-. 2. Authors, Canadian (English)--20th century--Biography. 3. Gimli (Man.)--Social life and customs. 4. Gimli (Man.)--Biography. 5. Autobiographies. I. Title.

PS8551.R765Z46 2017   C813'.54   C2017-904366-8
                                                C2017-904367-6

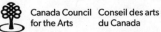

Contents

For Dylan Hall and Jackson Friesen:
The Next Generation

Prelude: Truth and Memory

The past is not something that is still "out there." Events occur in time and they vanish the moment they occur. The critic Jacques Derrida points out that the most we can say about any event is that it refers to a time that was once a present but is no longer a present. The past in all its complexity can never be reclaimed. It cannot be visited. All we have of the past are traces that indicate that something once occurred.

I've always been puzzled by the statement, "based on a true story." A narrative may be based on actual events or it may be based on a story, but it cannot be both. There is no underlying truth. There is always only a story. And it may or may not be believable, but it is never true in any fundamental way.

And for any writer that is a problem. The world is full of events, but these events are interesting only after a writer has given imaginative form to them. That is what I love about being a writer. I began writing with the idea that there were fictions I could write purely out of my imagination and they were different from memories and experiences. After a lifetime of writing and claiming that what I wrote were stories based on truth or that the things I wrote had nothing to do with me as a person, I have decided to come clean.

I write nothing but autobiography. However different the things are that happen in my writing, they all come from my memory, my imagination, my fantasies, my desires, and my experience. So what follows is a series of "true stories," though, like all stories, the only truth is that one mind invented them all.

In 1982 I published a book called *Fifty Stories and a Piece of Advice*. It was my first book of fiction. I was beginning to write and I had some radical ideas of how to go about it. I had dozens of ideas for stories. They were to be realistic stories about my life and the place I was from. I did not, however, want to sit down and mine my memory for stories. I decided to write the main story for the collection as a series of fragments, brief anecdotes that were at the heart of what I intended to write. The rest of the stories I thought of as five-finger exercises—experiments in different ways of telling a story. In this way I thought I could free myself from memory and move right into fiction.

Of course, nothing is that easy. There is no escaping memory, and it is impossible to write outside the conventions of narrative. If you want people to read you, they have to want to continue reading. The single most important thing is to make the reader want to read the next sentence. Anything can distract a reader: the rustle of trees in the wind, a distant explosion, the smell of stew cooking, the need to pee. And once your readers have gone, it is very difficult to get them back. The single greatest sin is boredom.

And so I offer you here a series of memory pieces rooted in a time and a landscape with which I am intimately familiar. Some of the places and practices that inform these essays may not be familiar to all readers, but I have always felt that one of the joys of reading is to be introduced to new places and ideas by good local guides. I will take you through my hometown, Gimli, and the regions thereabout. I will show you how to smoke fish, how to pick berries, and how to make jellies. I will introduce you to finding local herbs and using them in cooking. I will show you some of our local birds and animals, and take you to the Ice Carnival. I'll ask you to share Christmas with me. I will take you on a tour of Gimli's historic stores and for a ride on Winnipeg Beach's roller coaster. You'll meet some Icelanders and some Ukrainians. You'll take part in local sports, both in summer and winter, and I'll show you some very local games. I will introduce you to my mother and to a couple of my grandmothers, who will probably share some of their stories with you. As a special treat, we'll spend some time with a Nobel Prize winner. All this and a cast of hundreds. I will not, however, guarantee accuracy. This is not a work of history. If you want guarantees of a scientific sort, you will have to look elsewhere.

We'll begin with a visit to Willow Island and a brief history of New Iceland. We'll see some spectacular storms and maybe throw a few sandbags because of high water. Don't expect a proper history or any large helping of truth. I'm here to tell a story and show you the world I share with the people I love.

Willow Island is the stretch of land that looks like the south arm of Gimli bay. It is in fact an island joined by a causeway, and the lagoon behind it hides the actual shoreline. It has had quite a few different names since it was first recognized by explorers and settlers. The vagaries of the lake levels mean that it is sometimes a continuous stretch of land and sometimes a series of islands.

In 1800 Alexander Henry called it "Presqu'île," almost an island. It first appeared on a map in 1824 as Willow Island. In 1858 and 1860 it was variously mapped as Willow Point, Willow Isles, and Willow Islands. The Icelanders who settled here in 1875 called it "Vidines," which translates as "Willow Point."

When the Icelanders first arrived in 1875, they landed near a large white rock on the beach at Willow Island. There is considerable controversy over that landing, and first-hand reports differ. One version says the Hudson's Bay Company steamship, *The Colville,* towed the settlers on flatboats into the centre of the bay and cut them adrift so that they landed near the white rock. The most famous painting of the landing supports this version. Another version says that they were hauled into the lagoon and landed on the other side of the island, then made their way to land near the white rock. Supporters of each version cite reasons why it must have been one way or the other, but it is far too late to solve that mystery.

At any rate, the first baby born in "New Iceland," as they called the settlement, was born in the shelter of the white rock shortly after they landed. Even here there is some controversy about the date of the landing and the birth. Some accounts claim the landing took place on October 21, 1875, but other accounts set the date at October 22. Jon Johannson's birth certificate says he was born several days later. There is, however, a letter in the Canadian Archives, written by the leader of the expedition, John Taylor, and dated October 21, that describes the landing and the birth, and so that is likely the correct date.

Most of the settlers spent the first winter on Willow Island, though some may have begun to move to the centre of the bay at what is now Gimli. Gimli was named for the Great Hall of Gimli from the Elder Edda, where the best of gods, men, giants, and dwarves will dwell after Ragnarok, the end of the world in Icelandic mythology.

It was a tough winter. The settlers built rough log cabins chinked with clay and covered with tents loaned to them by the Hudson's Bay Company. Conditions were appalling. As many as twenty people shared each dwelling, and if the settlers were lucky, they also shared the space with a cow or two. Smallpox struck during the winter of 1876 and a third of the settlers, mostly infants and the elderly, died. My own grandmother was the first female child born in New Iceland, on February 14, 1876, just before the epidemic, but she survived and lived another ninety-nine years.

One of the earliest settlers to homestead on Willow Island was Gottskalk Sigfusson, known as "Gossi," and one of the bays on the island is named "Gosavik" after him. The well-known Olson family of Gimli descends from him. Eventually, he sold his homestead to my great-grandfather, Captain Baldi Anderson, a remarkable man who travelled all over North America, sold most of what is now Winnipeg Beach to the Canadian Pacific Railway (CPR) and built two hotels, one at Boundary Creek and the other in Gimli, each timed to open the day the railway arrived. He travelled with his dog team to Chicago in 1914 to take part in a silent film called *The Wild Goose Chase* and adopted and raised six children besides his own two.

In 1912 Willow Island was awarded a subdivision that still defines the structure of lots and roads in the present development. Captain Baldi was determined to start the development in the late twenties and early thirties. He foresaw the development of a row of cabins along a wooden boardwalk. He named the roadway "Marine Parade" and that is still its name on the official map of the subdivision. He thought the CPR would provide a new station stop where the Willow Island road meets Highway 9. He hired my father, his grandson, Baldwin Arnason, and together they loaded gravel onto a hayrack and built a road through the marshes to the beach. He optimistically named the beach "Captain Baldi's Bathing Beach," but he never earned a cent from his efforts.

After Captain Baldi's death, Willow Island passed to his son, Elli Anderson, who raised hay on the field at the end of the island, and sold sand and gravel for road building. In 1956 Elli offered to sell the place to my father, who was still inspired by Captain Baldi's vision. Dad and his brothers built a new road, cleared the land, set up tenting lots, built a couple of bathhouses and a store, erected a magnificent gate, and charged a dollar a car for anyone who wanted to go out to the wonderful shallow beaches with their sandy bottoms and sandbars.

During the period of the operation of the tourist resort, many of the tenters built elaborate tenting sites and came back year after year. Unfortunately, 1966 was a year of very high water and the road was severely damaged, so the resort had to be closed. The family did all it could to repair the damage, and Willow Island opened again in 1967. As a centennial project, the family raised the white rock, the main site for the memory of the New Icelanders, and turned it into a monument dedicated to their parents, Gudjon and Petrina Arnason. Every year Icelandic Canadians turn up on October 21 for the "Walk to the Rock," which celebrates the original landing.

The water remained high and in the end it became clear that the island was not a good investment as a tourist resort. The family decided to close the resort and divide up the land among its members. At first there were only family members, but as children grew up and moved away, they sold their lots to other people, and Willow Island is now a settlement not much different from other cottage developments.

After 1967 there were several years of very low water and the island returned to its original shape. Storms had separated the south shore, creating a new island. People who live there call it "Pelican Island," though soon it was no longer a separate island but an extension of Willow Island. The late seventies brought more devastation. The hydro development at Playgreen Lake meant that for several years high water was back, but that was followed by the drought of the eighties when the lagoon was almost too shallow for boats.

Willow Island has a way of healing itself. High water sometimes does damage, but the shoreline normally comes back, and land that seems lost after one storm returns after another. That wisdom has been strained after the storms of the last few years. The section called Pelican Island has been fragmented into a series of tiny islands. Willow Island has always been central to the history of Gimli and the memory of New Iceland. It is where this community was founded. Willow Island has been around for thousands of years, and we can only hope that the lake will once again heal itself and Willow Island will be whole again.

The Best of All Possible Worlds

First Arrivals:
The Settling of New Iceland and
the Myth of Beginnings

The first permanent settlement of Icelanders in North America was established in Gimli, Manitoba, October 21, 1875, at 4:30 p.m. On that day, the first day of winter according to the Icelandic calendar, 285 persons landed at Willow Point just south of the present site of Gimli, and by the evening of their arrival, the number had swelled to 286. The exact number, like many facts about the early settlement, is under dispute. Jon Johannson, or Jon å Bolstad, the first child, was born in the New World, and the land had thus been claimed.

The Icelandic settlement in Manitoba was unique in a number of ways, and the experience of the settlers was quite radically different from that of other ethnic groups that immigrated to the Canadian prairies. It was, to begin with, an apocalyptic event. A series of volcanic eruptions in Iceland between 1873 and 1875 had left nearly 5,000 Icelanders homeless. There was neither the room nor the economic base in Iceland during the following period of recession to absorb the displaced, and this, combined with an invitation from Governor General Lord Dufferin, led to a move to migrate to Canada. It is significant that the emigrants did not move primarily because of economic disadvantage, though certainly economic conditions were not good. Neither did they move in reaction to political or religious conditions at home. The group that left was heterogeneous. The poor and the wealthy alike, professionals, craftsmen, fishermen, and farmers all made the move together.

The Icelandic settlement was a representative slice of Icelandic society, not a single level, and in this way it was different from any other large group of settlers to come to Canada.

The Icelandic settlers chose to move to the shores of Lake Winnipeg for a number of reasons. Many of them were fishermen, and the lake was teeming with fish. The shores of Lake Winnipeg were heavily wooded and, for Icelanders whose own forests had completely disappeared, an inexhaustible supply of firewood and building materials seemed attractive. The government of Canada offered them a degree of independence that was quite striking but dependent on their settling in the district of Keewatin, north of the boundary of the postage-stamp province of Manitoba.

The details of the settlement, known as the "Icelandic Reserve" or the "Republic of New Iceland," depending on who refers to it, are unique. The Icelandic settlers were given an area about forty-two miles long and about eleven miles wide, stretching along the shores of Lake Winnipeg from

Boundary Creek at the site of the present Winnipeg Beach to the Icelandic River and including Hecla Island. Only Icelanders were permitted to settle in this area. The Icelanders were guaranteed the use of Icelandic as their official language in perpetuity. English criminal law was in effect, but the Icelanders were permitted to use their own civil law, which they did, writing a charter that was distinctly different from either English or Icelandic law. It has, for example, an elaborate system of social welfare and support for widows and the indigent. The franchise was extended to all gainfully employed men of good character over the age of eighteen. All men over the age of twenty-one years, except for schoolteachers and ministers of the gospel, were eligible for office.

The entire district was called "Vatnsping" or "Lake Country." The myth of beginnings is important for understanding the experience of the Icelandic community. Other prairie communities were named after people (MacGregor, McCreary) or Old Country places (Balmoral, Sans Souci), or Indigenous place names (Winnipeg, Pinawa). Gimli, the site of the first settlement, was named for the Great Hall of Gimli in Norse mythology. The Elder Edda tells us that after Ragnarok, when Fenrir kills Odin and the wolves Skoll and Hati eat the sun and the moon, when Yggdrasil, the world ash, is shaken, and the gods are defeated in final battle, all the universe will return to fire and sea. Out of that will arise an island on which will be situated the Great Hall of Gimli. All the best of men, of giants, of gods, and the creatures of outer darkness will be gathered here. (It's a tough place to get into: only a few gods will make it.) That post-apocalyptic vision is a perfect naming for people whose homes have literally disappeared under fire.

Let me tell you the story as it is told to children of the community. The Icelanders left their homes because erupting volcanoes drove them into the icy sea. They travelled for months in terrible hardship across the ocean. When they arrived in Canada, nothing was ready for them. They spent a year in Kinmount, Ontario, before heading west. They crossed Lake Superior in a fierce storm, then made their way to Duluth, then continued over to Fisher's Landing on the Red River and down to Winnipeg. There they hired three barges, enormous flatboats, which they dragged down the river until they reached the mouth. They were met by the Hudson's Bay Company steamer, *The Colville,* the only steamer on Lake Winnipeg. They were on their way to the Icelandic River, but it was late in the year and a fall storm came up. The captain cut the barges adrift and they floated in to shore.

They landed by a giant white rock, the only large white rock on the south side of Lake Winnipeg, and the first Icelandic baby in the New World was born there in the shelter of the rock. The first winter was the coldest winter in history, and the settlers lived in tents given to them by the Hudson's Bay Company and rough log cabins they built, although it was so late in the season that the ground was frozen and they had trouble finding mud to chink the cracks. It was a difficult time for these settlers. They were unused to axes. Iceland had almost no trees. They didn't know how to fish under the ice. In Iceland the ocean didn't freeze.

The next summer there was a great smallpox epidemic and 102 people died. The epidemic lasted for over a year and the community was tested by isolation and fear when it was quarantined. No one was allowed in or out. Families were separated and there was almost no help for the dying. Over the next twelve years, there were nine years of flood and a plague of locusts. It should have been the end, but it wasn't. The people named all the farms, more settlers came, and the community thrived.

Most of the story told to the children is factually true, but more important, it is also mythically true. Both metaphorically and literally cut adrift, the Icelanders make an accidental landing at the wrong place, which is nevertheless signalled to be the proper place by the miraculous white rock. They face a purification by disease, a testing by flood, a plague of locusts, and an act of naming. They undergo the same process of claiming a country that is described in the old Icelandic *Landnamabok*, the book that describes the discovery of Iceland.

So the Icelanders who moved to Manitoba played out a version of the founding of Iceland in their founding of New Iceland. They settled on Lake Winnipeg. It would be easy to argue that Icelanders are fishermen and so they chose to live on a lake. But they were not lake fishermen. They had to learn to fish all over again, setting nets instead of trolling them, fishing at least for part of the time through a metre of ice. They were taught to fish by the Indigenous people and they developed a very special relationship with them through that experience.

The floods that wiped out their work again and again were accepted as necessary and inescapable, a new testing. The more practical Ukrainians who came after 1897 immediately dismantled the beaver dams on the ridge west of the settlement, which were the cause of the flooding, and put an end to it.

The truth of some of my details might be disputed. Perhaps

things did not happen in just such a way. In fact, the Icelanders were probably not cut adrift and left to land in the storm. More likely, they were hauled through the channel to the quiet waters of the lagoon behind Willow Point. But I'm not interested in some narrow historic truth here. I'm more interested in a good, serviceable, mythic truth. The Republic of New Iceland lasted for twelve years, from 1875 to 1887. It was not an actual republic, but that is the name that Icelanders later came to use to refer to the Icelandic Reserve. It was incorporated into an expanded Manitoba in 1881, but it didn't lose all its special rights immediately. It maintained its system of government until 1887. Only Icelanders were allowed into the area until 1897, when it was finally opened to other settlers. The new settlers turned out to be mostly Ukrainian and Polish, peasants with a feel for farming. The Icelandic settlement became basically urban. There was no equivalent in Iceland for the large isolated farm, and when the Ukrainian farmers arrived, many of the Icelanders breathed a sigh of relief, sold off their homesteads, and moved into towns and cities. They largely abandoned the countryside to the Ukrainians. This turned out to be a workable system. The Ukrainians who came were a socially uniform group. They were only farmers. The Icelanders became the group of merchants who served the community.

The Icelandic community is one of the oldest ethnic immigrant communities on the prairies. Only the Mennonites who arrived at about the same time have as long a history. And yet, in spite of the fact that the communities have largely dispersed, and that the old settlements like Gimli and Riverton and Arborg are no longer largely Icelandic, there continues to exist a large and vital Icelandic presence on the prairies.

The Icelanders continue to publish a newspaper. They have several active cultural institutions such as the Icelandic Fron and the Icelandic National League of North America.

Where later immigrants to Manitoba, such as the Norwegians, the Swedes, and the Germans, have largely been so integrated that there is little sign of their cultural presence, the Icelanders continue to form a significant cultural group. The source of this cohesiveness is the myth of beginnings, a myth shared by Icelandic Canadians and Icelandic Americans as well. We look backward, not to some lost haven across the sea in Iceland, but to our roots as a people in a new land. When we hold our celebrations, we honour the Old Country but we celebrate the New as well. When we tell our epic stories, they are stories located in the New Land, stories like the horrors of the smallpox epidemic, when the bodies of children were stacked on the roofs of houses so that wolves would not get at them until they could be buried in the spring. Or even lighter stories, like the marriage of Caroline Taylor and Sigurdur Kristofersson, which took place on Netley Creek, the happy couple on one side and the Métis minister in a boat in the middle of the creek, shouting out the ceremony. We even have our own anthem, Guttormur J. Guttormson's poem "Sandy Bar," a powerful evocation of the sadness of pioneer experience, and a poem more important to Icelanders in North America than any of the great Icelandic medieval epics.

And finally, we have our own carnival, our special celebration, Islendingadagurinn. For many years, it has been the central event of the Icelandic experience in North America. Firmly located in time and space (Gimli, the first Monday of August), it is the focal point of our thinking of ourselves as a group. Here, we are ruled by our Fjallkona, the Maid of the Mountain, not some young girl, but an older woman, earth mother, celebrated for her contribution to the community as a whole. It is a wonderful and entirely unique position, a creation of the community here and not an imported ceremony from Iceland. (The Fjallkona had been a somewhat different figure in earlier ceremonies in Iceland, though the role had pretty much disappeared there. Her success in the New World revitalized her as a figure in Iceland.)

At Islendingadagurinn we gather from all over the continent, we renew acquaintances, we hold family reunions, and, most importantly, we renew the myth of our beginnings, and in that myth we find a sense of community that holds together a dispersed people who have entered thoroughly into the national mythologies of Canada and the United States. Because of the hold of that myth, it is possible to think of yourself as a New Icelander even if you speak no Icelandic and have never been to Iceland.

Even more importantly, the myth of beginnings ties together the Icelandic community of North America with the other communities of Manitoba that help us to celebrate. For the Ukrainians, the Poles, the British, the Germans, and all the other races and groups that make up the community of the Interlake, the founding myth is also their story. Islendingadagurinn is also their celebration. As contemporary North Americans, we live in many cultures at the same time. We wish to protect our own, but also to share it. Islendingadagurinn and the myth of beginnings it celebrates is important to Canada. It gives us one more valid way of being Canadian without evoking ancient dreams of Europe.

Icelanders and Ukrainians

Anyone who grew up in the Interlake before the late 1950s could be excused for believing that the world consisted of Icelanders and Ukrainians with a smattering of other ethnic groups. There were, of course, Poles and Germans and Jews, but the language of commerce was either Icelandic or Ukrainian. Those were the languages we listened to in stores, though most people could also speak a fairly heavily accented English.

The Icelanders were the first immigrants here, arriving in 1875. The Ukrainians came a bit later, in 1898. My grandfather remembered the first of them. He said that he was seven years old when his mother pointed out a team of oxen pulling a cart wagon with a Ukrainian couple and a bunch of children. His mother sent him out with a pail of milk for the new neighbours. An auspicious beginning.

Things weren't always so congenial, and there were tensions between the groups. The Ukrainians had been peasants

11

in the Old Country and were excellent farmers. The Icelanders had been mostly fishermen and urban dwellers. Things stayed that way for quite some time, with the Ukrainians buying out the homesteads of Icelanders who moved into the towns and began businesses.

By the time I was in high school the groups had begun to integrate. They married each other, they celebrated together, and they formed partnerships. Many of my friends were Ukrainians and I celebrated Ukrainian Christmas and Ukrainian Easter with them. Since the Ukrainians followed the Gregorian calendar and the Icelanders the Julian, we had the best of both worlds. Two Christmases and two Easters to celebrate each year.

I grew up and kept my friends, and I still cherish them. I became a writer and had the good fortune to be invited to do a tour of Ukraine and Russia along with writers Robert Kroetsch and Dennis Cooley. The Ukraine I had imagined was the peasant Ukraine of the nineteenth century. The Ukraine I discovered was quite a different thing, and it affected the things I wrote and my whole idea of the Slavic people. We landed in Kiev in the spring of 1991, just as the communist system was in crisis. I spoke neither Russian nor Ukrainian but fortunately our organizer and guide was Stella Hryniuk, who was fluent in both languages.

The Kiev airport was not a great advertisement for communism. It was simply a large concrete bunker with a leaky roof. I had, of course, read the various American and Canadian articles that pointed out the crippling poverty and squalid conditions in Russia and Ukraine. And there was some truth to that view, but no one pointed out the stunning beauty of the country and the elegance of the people.

The Ukrainians were supposed to have left an impoverished country. And yet, as we drove through the countryside we saw incredibly rich fields of wheat, topsoil so deep we have nothing to compare in Canada.

Stella had made arrangements with a Canada–Ukraine friendship organization, and we were treated very well. Everywhere we travelled we were feted and fed royally. We met writers and students and professors and publishers. Our first surprise was how well everyone was dressed. Secretaries looked as if they were on their way to a wedding. People wore leather pants and skirts and jackets. The buildings were heated by ceramic furnaces that were works of art in their own right. Meetings started at eight o'clock in the morning. And they always started with toasts of vodka and cognac. As the day went on we had to be very careful of the amount of alcohol we were expected to consume. I damaged a huge number of potted plants each day before the real partying began.

Ukrainian artists were taken seriously. It was a great honour to be a poet, and the state supplied living wages for writers, poets, actors, and painters. Books of poetry were published in the hundreds of thousands of copies. A lot of our work was translated into Ukrainian and published, though the publishers were unable to pay us royalties.

Instead, we got to travel from Kiev to Odessa and to Lviv, Ternopil, and Chernivtsi. We swam in the Black Sea and we met a huge number of artists. We travelled into the Carpathian Mountains and had a picnic with the health minister of the oblast, who was himself a well-known poet. We visited collective farms and churches and graveyards. We visited the grave of Taras Shevchenko, Ukraine's answer to Shakespeare.

And we were given a tour of the Odessa Catacombs by two beautiful young women, both named Tanya. They showed us where the Nazi forces had slaughtered the Ukrainian resistance fighters during the last week of the war. We visited Babi Yar, the mass grave where hundreds of Ukrainian Jews died. It was a place of haunting beauty and sadness, a place that I had wanted for a long time to visit.

We got no royalties but we were treated royally, and I fell in love with a country of beauty and passion. The events in Ukraine right now make me very sad, but I'm sure the Ukrainians will come through all right. They always do.

Three Mothers

It's a bright March day, colder than it should be but still not very cold. The sun glistens on the snow that fell all day yesterday and then through the night. My grandmother was born here 142 years ago, but I have no idea what the weather was like. Probably something like today. Her name was Gudrun Helga Hallgrimsdottir, and she was the first Icelandic girl born in New Iceland.

Everybody came down with smallpox. Well, not everyone but pretty close. Her two older sisters had it and came out marked, but my grandmother was somehow immune through all that tragic winter. It was mostly infants and old people who actually died, and because the ground was frozen and there was no way of burying them, their bodies were piled on the roofs of the makeshift huts they lived in. That was so the wolves wouldn't eat them before spring came and they could be planted in the earth.

That's the story my mother told me, and I believe it.

Gudrun Helga Hallgrimsdottir. Photo courtesy of David Arnason.

Looking out over the lake from where I sit, it is easy to believe that you are at the North Pole and nobody else exists in the whole world. The wind from the north churns up swirls of snow and forms drifts along the treeline.

My mother knew a verse in Cree that one of the children from the reserve near where she lived taught her on the way to school. She said she thought it was a dirty verse, because he laughed when she recited it aloud. She never forgot it and after she taught it to me, I never forgot it either. I know some Cree speakers but I don't dare recite the verse for them, because it might just be nonsense, or so corrupted by my mother's memory and then my own that it might make no sense.

My mother, Gudrun Anna Arnason, died on December 2, 1991. She had lived a life almost entirely defined by her family. Almost entirely but not quite. She was born in Libau, Manitoba in 1915, the third youngest in a family of eleven children, and named for her mother. She attended the Sheffield school, a one-room country school in Poplar Park that went up only to grade eight. She had a nimble mind and at the age of eleven found herself having skipped two grades and completed the entire curriculum. She couldn't go on to high school until she was twelve, so she spent a year out of school. She remembered that year as one of the most enjoyable in her life, but also as the loneliest. She didn't get to see and play with the friends she had left in school, but she did get to read a lot and she read voluminously. Her father had been a schoolteacher turned farmer who collected books, and in that year of grace delivered to her by the school system, she read through his library.

Her father's death a couple of years earlier had caught

everyone by surprise and altered all their lives. He had been relatively well-to-do, the man who had the first radio in the district, the first electric lights, a large house purchased from the T. Eaton Company, and a yacht on the river.

His records from shortly before his death indicate that his financial situation was excellent, but he was, for whatever reason, depressed, and he ended his life by his own hand. My grandmother and the older sons took over the running of the farm, but by then the Depression of the thirties was just about to arrive, and nothing was safe. Certainly not the stocks in the Cunard Line my grandfather had left as a legacy. His small fortune was converted overnight into worthless paper.

Still, my mother's meteoric academic career as a young scholar had given the family expectations for her, and her brothers and her mother were determined that it would carry on. They sent her to the Jon Bjarnason Academy in Winnipeg, an Icelandic private school that also educated some of the children of the wealthiest and most established Winnipeg families. The family made an enormous sacrifice to pay her dues and her room and board, and my mother did not disappoint them. She did brilliantly in school but the Depression deepened and the funds to keep her dried up. She found herself at fifteen having completed grade eleven and eligible to go to the university, but with little more before her than a future as a domestic servant. She went back to Libau and the farm and waited.

I don't want to make this appear tragic. There was very little money and nothing approaching a career, but everyone was in the same boat. The young people of Libau made their own fun. They put on dances. They started a little newspaper. They went swimming in the summer and skating in the

Petrina Thorunn Soffia Arnason. Photo courtesy of
David Arnason.

winter. Great things were abroad in the world, and the time
passed agreeably.

A couple of years later she found a job in Gimli working for a bookmaker who made beautiful hand-decorated,
leather-covered books. He was always called "old Bookmaker," and though he must have had some other name, I
have been unable to discover it. A couple of years later she
was offered a job at the Betel Personal Care Home in Gimli

and she seized the chance. The few other jobs she had found working for women not much richer than she were enough to convince her that a steady job was something she wanted.

The rest seems simple. She married my father, settled into a house in the country, and raised seven children. Her life might appear as the endless round of the domestic servitude she had feared and to which she seemed doomed. But she never forgot her academic interests. She read incessantly right until her health failed shortly before her death.

Our house was filled with books. Mother gave up much to raise her seven children but she insisted on keeping a membership in the Book of the Month Club. She somehow found the money to buy novels and poetry and books on science and politics. "Read," she told her children. "The life of the mind is as important as the details of the everyday world." And she proved it with stories about medieval times, about the reign of Queen Elizabeth I, about the American South before the Civil War, and about the aristocratic old Ontario of the *Jalna* novels. She read stories set on sailing ships in the tropical South or the Arctic North or the mysterious Chinese East. When we asked why she didn't want to go to these places, she answered only, "Cows can travel."

I've been to some of those places since, and I think she was right. The actual landscape of Fiji does not measure up to the Fiji of my youthful imagination. London is full of travellers in suits occupying the spaces where there ought to be stagecoaches and pickpockets and nineteenth-century fogs.

So I don't feel sorry for Mother. She might have been a doctor or a lawyer or a writer herself. She might have been a famous traveller. But she took the hand the world dealt her and she made the most of it. She balanced a life of domestic detail with a life of the active mind, and she passed her enthusiasm for ideas on to her children. Shortly before she died, she told me that if she had her life to live over, she wouldn't change a minute of it. And whenever I get into a discussion of the limitations of women's lives, or men's lives, for that matter, I remember her words: cows can travel.

Her mother, my maternal grandmother, died in 1964. She was eighty-eight years old. The night she died I went to the beer parlour in Libau with many of the mourners, including my uncle Bill, who lived with her and took care of her. Almost everybody there was related to me. In a flurry of coats and goodbyes, everyone left. And then there were only the two of us. He didn't want to go back to the house where his mother had died, so I took him home with me to Transcona, where I lived at the time. The next day I took Bill to the planetarium and then to the art gallery. When I finally brought him home to Libau a few days later, everybody was upset because no one knew what had happened to him. Now he's dead too, and I'm sorry I made everyone worry.

Last year I lived for several months in Kiel, Germany. The weather wasn't much better than it is here in Gimli. But I was happy because nothing in Kiel triggered memories. Everything was brand new and none of it was tied to a past that meant anything to me. We travelled all around Europe in the wonderful trains and we visited cathedrals laden with history, but it was somebody else's history and so it did not weigh on me.

My grandmother's house had a parlour, a room reserved for special visitors. It held an old piano that was hopelessly out of tune and one of those strange desks with hundreds of tiny drawers and a curved, slatted front cover that went up and down. There was a small chesterfield with an anti-macassar, and my grandfather's books, untouched since the day he put a shotgun in his mouth and pulled the trigger some fathomless time ago. I used to go to his grave on a summer's day and marvel at the granite slab that marked it. It was only years later that I learned that the granite slab marked his father, and my grandfather was in a grave nearby, marked only by a row of white stones.

After my grandfather's death, life for the family became very difficult. My grandfather, Thorsteinn Andres Anderson, had been a fairly rich man. He had a farm with many animals. He had built a large house on the prairie, and though electricity had not yet arrived in Libau, he had a gasoline generator. At night he lit up the house like a lantern, and people came from miles around to see it, a beacon in the dark prairie marshes.

I remember as a child our trips to Libau. On the way we passed through Winnipeg Beach, where someone had created a private cemetery with a white stone angel. My parents were not religious and they had some difficulty explaining to me just what an angel was. Later, the teachers in school provided their own explanations, complete with sheets of paper with angels you could colour with your crayons. That didn't help much, because I always had trouble staying within the lines. I still do. And I could never figure out what colour an angel should be.

My Libau grandfather died years before my visits, and my grandmother had retreated into silence. She had given up speaking English, and even though my mother and her brothers and sisters could speak Icelandic, my grandmother replied in monosyllables. She was a terrifying figure to me as a child, because she dressed in black and her silence gave her power.

My mother grew sweet peas in her garden. My father planted wooden stakes, then wove a web of string for the sweet peas to climb. On the south side of the house she grew hollyhocks, red and yellow and white. There was a plum tree in the bush near the house, and my mother picked it to make jam every September. She planted two small spruce trees in the curved flowerbeds near the road, one for me and one for my brother. They are still there, though many other families have grown up in that same place.

We had a ghost. Her name was Rikka, and she had come from Iceland around the turn of the century. My mother had nursed her in the Betel nursing home, and she came to live with us when I was only about three. I remember her with her long grey hair braided, sitting in a rocking chair and singing to herself. She had a picture of the baby she gave birth to in Iceland, who had died before he was a year old. I didn't know at that time that death came to children, and it was a frightening revelation. She ate oatmeal porridge with brown sugar, and she broke up pieces of toast into her cereal. Then one day she was simply gone. No one explained to us what had happened, and we didn't ask in case she had died. Now there is no one to ask.

One spring several years after Rikka left us, my mother was doing her spring cleaning and she asked me to bring several boxes of books from the basement. Rikka had given them to Mother with the stipulation that she take special care of them. The basement had flooded that winter, and though none of the books were soaked, they all smelled of mould. Mother made a fire and piled a batch of books on it. I carried boxes of books from the basement to feed the flames. I had a rake with me to stir the fire and I used it to pull one of the volumes out to look at it. Several banknotes blew out over the snow. I grabbed a few and showed them to Mother. She pulled all the books out of the fire, and we went through them. Many of them had four-dollar bills between the leaves, and when we were done we had gathered just over $500. Remember that this was just after World War II. $500 was an enormous amount of money. My father had just completed building our house. It had cost $500.

I fell hopelessly in love in the first grade with a bossy little girl named Irene. She always made me carry her books home, though she lived only a couple of blocks north of the school and I lived three kilometres away in the country south of town. I was always thrice adreams those days and though my parents knew my penchant for getting lost in daydreams, they became worried when I didn't get home until well after dark.

Then one day I was told I could go home with Irene and play with her until nine o'clock, when my parents would pick me up. We played all sorts of games, all of them of her invention and all of which involved her dominating me in subtle ways. The next day at school she did not appear. She was missing for a whole week. Finally I asked a classmate about her, and he told me that she had moved away to Winnipegosis. I still fall in love with bossy girls.

My father's mother, Petrina Thorunn Soffia Arnason, was born on the 10th of March, 1896. Her mother, Petrina Soffia Arngrimsdottir, died nine days later. She was twenty years old. My great-grandfather, Captain Baldi Anderson, was dismayed at the death of his wife and bewildered about what to do with an infant child. He took his daughter to a woman he knew and asked her if she would raise the child. The woman agreed. Captain Baldi went home, but as the days passed he knew he couldn't give his child away, and so he took her back. He spent the rest of his life gathering lost children and raising them. He remarried, a woman named Elin Gisladottir, known as Lina, and had one son, Elli, with her. So my grandmother had a half-brother and two mothers.

My grandmother died just days before her ninety-ninth birthday after a lifetime of such relentless optimism and good humour that she came as close to saintliness as anyone I have ever met. She married my grandfather, who lived on the farm next door, when she was fifteen, and she raised ten children.

She defined herself so thoroughly as a farmer that she could not think of any other kind of life. She couldn't imagine why anyone would want to do anything other than farm. She told me once that her very first memory was of playing as a child with a pile of bones she had found. The larger bones represented the farmhouse and the barn. The medium bones were horses and cattle. The smallest bones were chickens.

And when she went on to farm herself, she took on what must have been back-breaking labour as if it were some wonderful game she was being allowed to play. She raised hundreds of chickens and sold their eggs and slaughtered the older ones for meat.

My grandfather had a large dairy herd, and she took part in milking, both morning and night. She slopped pigs, carried pails of milk, pitched in with the haying, and sang joyously, though tunelessly, most of the time. She and my grandfather walked in the fields nearly every night in summer to "watch the grain growing," as they put it.

And she loved animals. She knew all the horses and cattle by name, and she welcomed stray dogs and cats and made them part of the family. Once, however, she was attacked and injured by a heifer that had just given birth to a calf. The heifer had not yet been dehorned, and when her calf was taken away from her, she went a little mad. When she was being driven to the barn for her first milking, she suddenly attacked my grandmother and threw her into the air on the ends of her horns.

My grandmother would not be taken to the hospital. She calmed the heifer, got it into its stall, and milked it. Then she went to the hospital to discover that she had only a couple of broken ribs and some severe bruises. The next day she was back milking, insisting that she alone could keep the heifer calm. She cooed to it and stroked it and it came to be one of the best milkers in the barn.

It is hard to believe the world could ever have been as innocent as she describes. She said that it was not uncommon for strange men travelling down the road to knock on the door and ask for lodging. Even when her husband was away fishing on the lake, she would invite them in and give them food and a bed. No man, she said, did her any harm, and none was so much as impolite. She said she trusted that people were basically good, and if you treated them well, they would do the same for you. She claimed that she had never in her life been cheated. Maybe she was only lucky, but ninety-nine years is a lot of luck.

She yearned for the mother she had never seen, and she loved the mother who raised her. She knew of her birth mother only through a hand-tinted portrait of a young woman of fifteen with long black hair that hung to her waist.

Gudrun Helga Hallgrimssdottir Anderson. Photo courtesy of David Arnason.

David Arnason

She knew Lina as the warm-hearted woman who took in all the people both she and her husband, Captain Baldi, brought home.

My grandmother told me this story: One day, when she was about six years old and her family was living in Boundary Creek, now Winnipeg Beach, a little girl of about her age named Joa came over to ask for milk to feed the baby. Her mother, Solveig, was dying and the man they lived with didn't know what to do. Lina went right over and brought the three-month-old baby Bessi home, and Joa in the bargain. When the mother died a couple of weeks later, she left a bible with an inscription in it saying that baby Bessi was a gift to Lina, but that relatives would come to get Joa. The relatives never arrived, and so Lina kept both children. Then Lina's young brother, Sam, ran away from home and joined them.

Meanwhile, Captain Baldi had answered an ad for a man with a dog team. When he arrived in Chicago he discovered that he was to act in a silent movie called *The Wild Goose Chase*. He played his role but decided that he could make a few extra dollars by going to the Lakehead and working as a stevedore, loading ships. He did that for a couple of months, then took a train back to Winnipeg.

On the way he found a woman in distress. Her husband had deserted her in Toronto. She had three little boys with her and was going to put them in a home while she tried to find work in Winnipeg. Captain Baldi took the baby and promised to give him back to her as soon as she was back on her feet. He gave her all the money he had and took the baby home to Gimli. He handed the baby to Lina, who accepted it as if it had all been planned. And the woman never returned. They raised the baby as their own.

Then Lina's sister died, leaving seven children, and so they took on a couple of more children. My grandmother felt no resentment towards this ever-increasing brood, which by then included her half brother, Elli. Nobody squabbled, she said. They all got along just fine.

Grandmother did piece together the story of her birth mother and namesake, Petrina Soffia. Petrina was born in Iceland in 1876, the daughter of Arngrimmur Gislason and his wife, Thorunn. Her father, known as Arngrimmur Molari, was one of Iceland's first and most important painters, but he died when she was eleven, leaving her to be raised by her mother and her aunt and uncle on the neighbouring farm. She was a bright and beautiful young woman, but there were a lot of people trying to make a living on a small farm, and so when a well-to-do older farmer down the valley offered to marry her, she was faced with a dilemma. If she refused, she would be a burden to her relatives. So one day, she packed her bags, walked the twenty kilometres to Akureyri, and got on a boat bound for Canada. Three years later she married Captain Baldi, gave birth to my grandmother, and died nine days later from complications of childbirth.

She had good reason for leaving Iceland. She had the example of her mother, Thorunn Hjorleifssdottir. Thorunn had made the mistake of getting pregnant by a married man, the painter Arngrimmur Gislason. She was the daughter of the minister Hjorleifur Guttormsson, and one of nine girls in the family. It was, of course, a scandal, and to save face, she was married to an elderly farmer who lived down the valley. She bore him two sons, neither of whom survived, and after his death she married Arngrimmur, whose own wife had died in the meanwhile.

And I suppose that is why I am telling you all this. The amplitude of these anecdotes is proportional to their distance from me in time. I think I am growing old, and I don't want to. I have been blindsided by life. Just moments ago everything was expectation. I had plans. I lived in many different futures in my imagination, and I slept well at night and dreamed dreams of power and success. Now, I want to live in the past. I would be willing to live my life over exactly as it happened, taking the good with the bad, as if it were a favourite movie that I could replay whenever I wanted.

But of course life doesn't do you that sort of favour. I remember riding an Icelandic horse high in the mountains of Iceland. The trip was seventeen kilometres, and the highest eight were in deep snow. We followed an ancient trail marked by cairns and the horses took us through a landscape so rough and jagged I would never have set out on it if I had known in advance what to expect. Still, every moment of that ride is as fresh in my mind as if it had just happened.

I look forward to spring, though it will take me to my birthday and to the knowledge that I cannot recover all those things I have lost. My unplanned future is hurtling towards me and I am helpless to resist it. Lately, I have begun to dream of houses with secret rooms that contain artifacts from the nineteenth century—gas lamps and old irons and lockets with pictures of beautiful women carved in ivory. I am unreasonably happy in these dreams, and when I waken from one of them I am desperate to recover it.

Sometimes my children arrive in my dreams in the guises of their former selves, but never as they are now that they have moved on and made their own lives. Sometimes I am a child myself, and those are the most troubling dreams.

Once, my brother and I found eight puppies in a brush pile in the spruce bush across the road from where we lived. The mother was a yellow dog of indeterminate breed and she let us approach and pet the puppies. In memory this is one of the happiest moments of my life, but in dreams I am full of trepidation. I sense how powerless I am to save those pups, though in real life we did save them, bringing them home to Mother and finding new homes for them all.

Rabbits. I remember rabbits in the bush near home. I set snares for them and skinned them for their fur, and Mother cooked them and we ate rabbit stew. They seemed distant and other then, deserving of their fates, but now I have rabbits living in the backyard of my house in Winnipeg and I am concerned about them, fearful of dogs on the loose and feral cats. I have given them names and learned to identify one from the other. I bring them food, sunflower seeds and rabbit pellets and sometimes rye bread. They have become so tame that I can walk close to them and they will not move. It bothers me that they are so trusting.

Since I was young I have wanted to buy a convertible and drive through our too-short summers with the top down. I always thought that I would get one, some time in the near future. I rented one in California and drove through the starry desert night in February and I was happy. But I have not yet bought one, and it looks as if I probably never will. It was a small dream and easily realizable, and yet it failed and continues to fail me.

I should make lists, try to figure out what I want and what I need and put my life in order. But I know that I would lose the lists, that the priorities I set would never arrive in the correct order. I know because I have tried. I have bought electronic organizers and failed even to learn how to use them. I miss important meetings and forget about important dates. Yet, if I do remember, I am always punctually on time.

And meanwhile, important events occur. Countries go to war and thousands are slaughtered in the most inhumane ways. Innocent people are tortured together with the guilty without anyone much noticing the difference. Whole galaxies are spinning out of control. Black holes in space are swallowing stars and sending them into some unimaginable other place. And there is nothing I can do about any of it.

None of these events or people exist anymore. All that remains is memory. But memory can be reshaped by story, and the dead can be given a kind of new life. In 1990 I was in Iceland filming a documentary about my great-grand-mother, Petrina Soffia Arngrimsdottir, and I interviewed the Icelandic president, Vigdis Finnbogadottir. I asked her about Iceland's fascination with genealogy. She told me, "We are a tiny country. We need all the people we can get, including the dead." I have taken her words to heart.

A Fish Story

Igrew up on the shores of Lake Winnipeg, and, like most of my friends, my life has always been intertwined with fish and fishing. My father was a fisherman when he was young, and my memories are of skiffs parked in our yard and nets hanging from the joists in our basement. The nets were preserved with bluestone, copper sulfate, which kept them from rotting in the lake. The smell of the bluestone was heady and it suffuses all memories of my youth. As children, we would bury our faces in the nets until we were dizzy from the copper smell. It was almost certainly toxic, but probably no more than the gasoline we used to sniff from the outboard motors.

I was a child of the Second World War, and the world that I remember is hardly imaginable today. It was a rural world inhabited by animals: horses and cows, pigs and chickens, sheep and foxes, dogs and wolves and birds. The migrations every spring and fall darkened the skies. The bushes were filled with rabbits and groundhogs, gophers and squirrels and deer. Everywhere was abundance. There was simply more of everything in those days.

When the war ended my dad and his brother Joe bought four army-surplus Bren Gun Carriers. I remember the day they arrived, clanking into our farmyard on their metal tracks. My father, in what must have been some sort of late adolescent joy, drove one of them straight into the poplar bush, knocking down about a dozen fair-sized trees. The plan was to use the light tanks for fishing on the lake. A couple of these Bren Gun Carriers were converted into early versions of the Bombardiers that came to dominate the lake, but they were a bit too heavy and unmanageable for the task, and so they ended up hidden in the bush behind our house. They served perfectly for fantasies of warfare for my brother and our friends. The Bren Gun Carriers all had bullet holes right through the light armour, just where the driver would have sat.

But I wanted to talk about fish. They were the main part of our diet. We ate pickerel almost every day during the fishing season, pickerel with potatoes and green tomatoes, pickerel fillets with chives in season or with onions later in the year. Pickerel is a delicate fish that is best served fried in butter but without seasonings that mask its flavour. Every so often someone would call them walleyes, but nobody on the shores of Lake Winnipeg ever used that name. A cousin of the pickerel is the sauger, a smaller and darker fish that is nearly indistinguishable from the pickerel by taste. In Manitoba it is often sold as "baby pickerel" and is a bit more expensive. Perch is equally good and is easily available to anglers. It is smaller than pickerel or sauger, usually about 200 to 300 grams. Perch are easy to catch from the shore or from any dock that stretches out into Lake Winnipeg.

Fish, birds, and mammals often have local names that are quite different from the "official" names you will find in books. These distinctions can cause strong feelings, especially when someone insists that his name is the "real," "the correct," or the "official" name. Naming anything is no more than a convention, and there are no supreme authorities to choose one name above another. And that brings us to the sunfish. Books will tell you that what the locals call the sunfish is actually the freshwater drum. It probably got its name from the Icelandic *solfisk*, though some call it "silver bass." Whatever you call it, it was one of the fish I ate most often when I was growing up. It was usually served boiled. Cooked this way, it produced a black, almost slimy skin, but when the skin was removed it was quite delicious.

Another fish that was popular among the Icelandic population was the mariah, or maria, as we used to spell the name. The mariah is also known as the lingcod or the burbot, though, again, these names were never used by Lake Winnipeg fishermen. It is the only member of the cod family caught in fresh water and is widespread in the northern hemisphere, including Iceland. It has an enormous liver, about six times larger than the livers in other lake fish.

My grandmother had several recipes for this fish, and early Manitoba cookbooks sometimes mention it. The liver is supposed to be delicious, but though I tried cooking it in several recipes, it had a vile taste, exactly like cod liver oil, which is in fact what it is. The flesh, on the other hand, is delicious. It tastes very much like lobster. Unfortunately, the cod-liver-oil reputation has stuck to the fish and so there is very little market for it and most fishermen treat it as junk fish. Many fishermen do not like the feel of the soft belly and insist that

Gimli fishermen filleting fish. Archives of Manitoba, Gimli, Commercial Fishing 17(N18220).

it is a sort of snake. Still, if you can make friends with a fisherman, you might be able to buy a few pounds. I recommend it highly if lobster is a bit too much for your pocketbook.

When I was a child I was informed by my teachers that the goldeye grew only in Lake Winnipeg. The myth went that it was a prehistoric fish that had flourished in prehistoric Lake Agassiz and was isolated in Lake Winnipeg when Lake Agassiz dried up, leaving only lakes Winnipeg and Manitoba. A subset of the same legend held that they were also found in Lake Baikal in Russia. As it turns out, goldeye are found in lakes and streams throughout western Canada and the northern United States, and are now largely fished in northern Saskatchewan.

Another myth is that the fish tastes terrible if it is not smoked. In fact, like its cousin the mooneye, it can be scaled with little difficulty, stuffed with poultry dressing, and baked in an oven for about fifteen minutes. Both are fine-fleshed fish and both are delicious, a fact to which I can testify, having cooked them this way many times. Goldeye are most often smoked and for some strange reason dyed red, a procedure that adds nothing but an unnecessary chemical to the meal. I prefer the gold colour that my father achieved with his smoking.

A few years ago, in one of those fits of nostalgia that are usually best resisted, I decided to build a smokehouse and smoke my own fish. I could have bought a little electric smoker, but that would have felt like cheating, so I found a few old pieces of plywood and I built myself a smokehouse. I built it along a rarely used stretch of road allowance that had gone to bush where no one else was likely to stumble on it.

I built it in the shape of the old outhouses that used to decorate the landscape. It was about two metres high by one metre wide. All measurements are approximate because I was using old scraps of two-by-fours and plywood and some old, rusty nails I found in my garage. Still, after I had finished it, I was as proud as if I had constructed a mini Taj Mahal.

It had three full sides and one side that went up almost a metre to a makeshift door that could be removed. It had a sand floor with a small place for a fire in the centre. The roof was enough to keep out the rain, and the eaves would allow smoke to escape. I gathered some dry lilac sticks that I had saved a few years earlier for just such an occasion. I found some metal poles left over from a derelict television antenna to hold the fish.

I decided to begin my smoking career with goldeye, both because they are my favourite fish and because a fisherman friend of mine offered to donate about fifty goldeye and a dozen channel catfish to the project. The goldeye were frozen, which was just what I wanted. If you use fresh fish, they tend to fall from the rod on which they hang. I borrowed an old aluminum washtub from an uncle and made a brine. I put about two pounds of salt into the tub and added some water. Then I put a small potato into the tub and slowly added water until the potato floated, a time-honoured way of determining salinity. I cleaned and scaled the goldeyes, put them in the brine, and left them there overnight.

The next morning I started a fire in the centre of the smoke-house and let it burn for a couple of hours until it had burned down to coals. Then I mounded the coals into the shape of a volcano and covered them with wet sawdust, leaving a small hole to allow the smoke to exit and make its way between the fish and up to the gap in the eaves. I strung the fish on the rods, leaving enough space between each fish so that the smoke could do its work. I strung up the fish by pushing the rods through each fish's eye socket, then hanging the rods from the ceiling. Finally, I sat down on a lawn chair, opened a beer, and waited.

Coals under wet sawdust burn very slowly, and smoking fish is no pastime for the impatient. I left the fish for six hours of cold smoke. Then I dug the sawdust away from the coals and left the fish for a half hour of hot smoke. By that time the coals were nearly out, the fish were a wonderful golden brown, and the smell was intoxicating. All that was left was to eat a few fish, freeze a few more, and drive around town, offering fishy gifts to friends and neighbours.

A few days later I smoked the catfish. The procedure for smoking catfish is identical to the procedure for smoking goldeye, except that the fish is prepared somewhat differently. A catfish does not have a rib-like structure of bones. Instead, it has a central cartilaginous structure that acts as a spine.

My father had told me that the black coating that covers a catfish is bitter and should be removed by scraping with a sharp knife. On one occasion I forgot this step and regretted it later. He also said not to freeze the fillets, and he was correct about that as well. The oil in the catfish goes rancid after it has been frozen for a few weeks.

If you don't want to go to the trouble of smoking a catfish, one of the best methods of cooking is to prepare the fish Cajun-style. Fillet the lower part of the fish, remove the skin, and cut the fillet into pieces about one to two inches square. Roll the pieces in flour with Cajun spices (you can buy these or mix your own) and deep-fry the pieces. Cajun catfish can turn any suspicious guest into an immediate catfish fan.

A smaller cousin of the channel cat is the bullhead or mud pout. It is about as ugly as a fish can be. It is yellow and black with a large head with sharp spikes on each side and slimy whiskers. Bullheads are easy to catch, but not so easy to get off a hook without injuring yourself. Apparently in the period just around the Second World War, there was a large European demand for bullheads and they sold well, but they have since lost popularity and there is no significant fishery for them.

Like bullheads, suckers are a fish with few fans. They are bony bottom feeders, generally considered a coarse or garbage fish, and are often mistakenly called mullet. I have not eaten them myself, but my grandfather was a great fan. Once when I was a lot younger and he was in his early eighties, he complained to me that he had gotten too old and stiff. He could no longer fish for suckers, and it was impossible to buy them.

A couple of weeks later, in late May or early June of that year, I was driving home from the city. I stopped at Willow Creek to see if the jackfish were running. I saw no jackfish, but the creek was full of suckers. I thought immediately of my grandfather, but I was dressed in a suit and I had no way of catching fish. I walked down to the edge of the water and there on the shore was a large, heavy branch. I remembered that when I was in school, several of us would take large poles and slap the water above schools of suckers. Stunned fish would float belly-up on the water for a few minutes. I thought it was worth a try. I took off my jacket, rolled up my pants, picked up the stick, and waded into the creek. The first time I slapped the water, five fish rolled over, and I picked them up and threw them on the shore. Unfortunately, the water splashed up onto my suit, soaking me.

I was already wet with swampy creek water, so I waded deeper and continued my amateur fishing. A couple of cars stopped on the road above the creek and people asked what I was fishing for. Neither of the carloads was impressed with my catch of suckers. No one thought that suckers were edible. In the end I managed to collect twenty-eight fish, which I carried loose and flopping into the back of my new Volkswagen, something I should not have done. My grandfather was delighted with the suckers, which he put into a pail and carried into his house. My Volkswagen smelled of fish for the next couple of months. And I never did find out how Grandpa cooked them. Boiled them, I suppose. He could eat any fish boiled.

But that reminds me of another fishing adventure. My

grandfather lived on a farm across from a ditch that swelled every spring. It followed an old creek bed that led from Fish Lake, about twenty-five kilometres to the west, east to Lake Winnipeg. The ditch flowed under the railroad tracks through three culverts and on into the lagoon. One year the flood was particularly high, and jackfish poured through it on their way to the lake to spawn. My uncle Charley and I made a scoop from an old iron hoop and some chicken wire and settled in to fish.

The jacks arrived in huge numbers. Every time we set the scoop, we pulled out three or four fish. It was the 10th of May, I remember, because my cousin Brett was born that day. My uncle Frank was taking a turn with the fishing scoop when the doctor came by to tell him he had a son. The doctor took a turn with the scoop and wouldn't stop until his nurse came by and sent him back to the hospital.

People stopped along the highway to watch the fishing. A farmer who lived a couple of kilometres west asked if he could try. He soon had all the fish he could use. All that warm May afternoon, people went home to get boxes and pails to carry their largesse. Women and children arrived with picnic lunches, and the place began to look like a country fair.

Fishing was always a dangerous occupation. Like my father, most Lake Winnipeg fishermen could not swim. All the fishermen I knew had stories to tell of terrible storms in which they found themselves in gigantic waves that threatened to swamp their boats while they tried to find their way to shore in the darkness. My father told these stories and I listened to them as a child, fearing for his death every time he went out on the lake. Every year the obituaries described tragic drownings, and they still do.

Winter fishing was not much better. There was always the fear of falling through the ice, or getting caught in a blinding snowstorm and freezing to death. A few years ago I was staying in my studio at Willow Island, a few kilometres south of Gimli. I had gone cross-country skiing along the shoreline when a whiteout blew up. I managed to make it the few hundred metres back to the studio, grateful that I had not been farther into the lake. I lit my fireplace and turned on the powerful lights that shone over the lake so that I could watch the ferocity of the storm. I settled down to read, happy in my warmth, watching the snow build drifts right onto my deck.

This was just before Christmas, so it was completely dark before six o'clock. Towards midnight I heard a knocking at my door. I opened it to two fishermen so coated with snow that they looked like creatures out of a science fiction film. I invited them in, and they stood shivering by the door. Both were bearded and their beards were heavy with icicles. I recognized the older of the two as Roy Solmundson, who had been in the same grade with me at school and who was now a successful fisherman. The other man, I think, was his son-in-law. They had been out lifting their nets about fifteen kilometres from shore. They had been caught in the storm, unable to tell where they were. Their Bombardier took them a couple of kilometres in what they thought was the direction of the west shore, and then the engine quit.

They set off on foot. Roy told me he had remembered that the wind had been from the northwest so he kept his right cheek into the wind and started walking. They had been walking for several hours when they saw my lights, and a couple of hours more before they reached my door. I offered them each a glass of whisky but they refused. They wanted only to get home, where people would be waiting for them. My four-wheel-drive Dodge Durango made it through the deepening drifts, to all of our surprise. I dropped them off at Roy's place in Gimli, nearly as snow-covered as they had been when they knocked at my door.

In winter, one of the most important fish caught in Lake Winnipeg is the whitefish. It is prized for its white flesh and it has a large international market. Whitefish constitutes one of Manitoba's most important exports. Like goldeye and pickerel, it supports an industry that helps to define what it means to live on Lake Winnipeg. Whitefish is as popular with the local inhabitants as it is with the Americans and Europeans who are our market. It is enjoyed both smoked and cooked. From my childhood on, stuffed and baked whitefish was as central to my diet as roast beef is to the British, and it remains one of my favourite meals.

The lake is in danger today because of the pollutants in the runoff water that feeds from Lake Winnipeg's nearly two million square kilometres of watershed. Algae blooms foul the water that we drink, swim in, and use in a thousand different ways. And it is not only humans who are threatened. Bird, mammal, fish, and insect life, from the most advanced to the most miniscule, make their livings from the lake, and if it dies, we die with it. My dearest memories all derive from the lake. It will take an enormous effort to save Lake Winnipeg, but it is an effort we need to make.

Studio on the lake. Photo courtesy of David Arnason.

Living on the Lake

If you grew up in Gimli you will be haunted by Lake Winnipeg for the rest of your life. You will not be happy living without the sound of water, the cries of gulls, the thunder of waves, and the howling of wind. Other towns' beauty will be measured by their similarity to Gimli. Oceans can affect people as well, but oceans have a limited repertoire. They have really only one season, one voice, one limited palette.

But I've probably gone too far with that image. I've claimed more for Gimli than I can possibly sustain. It's not just Gimli. It's water in all its forms. There is something about water that affects and infects human imagination. People who live along rivers cannot imagine a decent life without rivers. Rivers become the metaphors that organize their lives and their memories. Rivers flow, they bend, they turn back on themselves. They bring things and carry them away. The Greek philosopher Heraclitus said that you can never enter the same river twice. The river you step into has already left you behind in its wanderings.

Lakes and rivers are inevitably tied to the marshes that surround them. Whatever the imaginative power of lakes, they are always fed and drained by rivers, but when the rivers slow and rest, the marshes take over. Here, the limpid clarity of lakes and the urgent rush of rivers give way to the slow, tumescent swell where life begins. Here, among the reeds and rushes, birds nest, frogs and fish lay their eggs, and the landscape is a ferment of creation. And there are other sources of water: ponds and creeks and sloughs and springs. The artesian wells where we got our water in Gimli hinted at a gigantic underwater lake where a whole other world went on without us.

My father was a fisherman. My early years were filled with the musty smell of blue-stoned nets and gasoline. My playthings were corks and leads and coils of rope and side line. I remember one fall day of storms when he appeared at the kitchen door dressed in his oilskins and rubber boots and dripping water onto the linoleum. He seemed ten feet tall, silhouetted against the door frame. Lightning lit up the sky behind him and thunder rumbled. I was terrified. I knew that I loved him, but at that moment I was terrified.

My father fished on Lake Winnipeg from the time he was fourteen until he was thirty-five. Like most of his contemporaries, he never learned to swim. I didn't learn to swim properly either, until I was in my mid-twenties. I spent several years taking courses until I had earned enough medals to qualify me as a lifeguard, but I still have no confidence outside a pool where I can reach out and touch the edges.

When I had nightmares, they were always about being swamped in a boat and drowning. I grew up listening to stories about fishermen being drowned either at work or on holidays with their loved ones. I knew the people who had drowned and I knew the people they had left behind.

At the same time, my dreams of plenty were always tied to the lake. I remember seeing boxes of brilliant fish, the bright white of sunfish and whitefish, the brilliant green of pickerel, the yellow of perch, and the black of catfish. In my dreams they appear as giant forms that float in the air or that I catch in nets and draw to shore.

I never liked fishing with a rod and reel. It always seemed to me somehow childish. When I was about five years old, I made my own rod out of a willow branch and a length of string with an open safety pin as my hook. One day my father brought home a box of carp, still alive and slapping in the box. He took them out to the back of our house and threw them in the slough. All summer my brother and I fished and a couple of times we even snagged an enormous carp, which we brought home to Mother, who quietly deposited it in the garbage.

In those days, our social lives were tied to the lake, at least in the summers. However the evenings began, they usually ended up with campfires along the lake. Somebody always had a guitar, and we sang and splashed until late in the night. There was not much alcohol. Sometimes someone might bring a six-pack of beer, but by the time it was shared among a dozen people, there was little chance of anyone getting drunk. That did not prevent the police from arriving suddenly out of the dark with their big flashlights, but since we already knew most of the police and they were not much older than we were, they were not very frightening. I suspect now that they wanted nothing more than to get out of their heavy uniforms, grab a beer, and join us on the sand.

Gimli had three overlapping populations. The first was the locals, people who lived there year-long, who had jobs and post office boxes and knew everybody. The other group was the cottagers, or "campers," as we called them, though nobody called a cottage a "camp." Each family in the camper group usually had one father who spent weekdays working in the city and who came out to relax on the weekend. That left a lot of lawns to be cut and cottages to be painted and repaired. The locals were convinced that all the campers were rich, and the campers were sure that the locals were out to fleece them. This made for a certain tension between the two groups, a tension that never came to outright hostility but was always there nonetheless.

The third group was the military, which divided itself into two groups; the airmen, who were single and lived in barracks; and the married couples who lived in the PMQs, the permanent married quarters. Their children thought of themselves as local, and they went to school with the local children. To the locals they were exotic, since they had lived all over the country and some of them had lived all over the world, but they became friends with the locals and many of them spent the rest of their lives in Gimli.

The airmen were a different matter. Gimli became a NATO training base, and hundreds of young men from all over the world came to learn how to fly, first on Mustangs and later on jet planes. After one group was trained, it was replaced by another: Italians and French, Norwegians and Swedes and Turks. This caused some difficulty because each new contingent of young men was interested in the local young women, and the local young men did not welcome the competition. There were a lot of fights between the airmen and the local boys, even though the senior officers at the airbase did as much as they could to calm things. By the late sixties the training program had ended and things went back to normal. Hundreds of people were touched by their sojourn near the lake, and many of them come back years later.

We hear now of the dangers to the lake, algae and mercury poison and pollution. The lake, scientists tell us, is dying. I don't like to have the lake quantified, for it to be no more than an ailing patient to be treated with chemicals. I know that they are right, and I do what I can to help. But it is the lake of memory and imagination that concerns me. That is the lake we love, and it is sustained by poems and stories and songs sung around campfires on beaches where we fall in love. That lake is in no danger as long as it exists in our communal imagination like a bright jewel we can always reach to make us happy.

Fall storm. Photo courtesy of David Arnason.

Christmas is filled with memory. Photo by Markus Spiske, pexels.com.
Brown and red horse decor hanged on Christmas tree 212311.

Christmas in Gimli

Christmas Day in Gimli was always bitterly cold, but the night sky was filled with stars and a pale moon shone through the dense spruce bush and the skeletal poplars. The snow had always just fallen and the drifts along the side of the road sparkled with diamonds. That, at least, is what I remember, and childhood memories are always better than ordinary truth.

I am thinking about a long time ago, the 1940s and '50s when I was young. There's not much good about growing old as the body starts to fail and is in constant need of repair, but the mind sifts through memories and polishes up the good ones and discards the unhappy ones. Living in the past is better than you might expect.

The Icelanders I grew up with doubled up on Christmas. Christmas Day was the day that some of us went to church and the others celebrated quietly at home with family. Christmas Eve was the time for opening presents and celebrations.

My family chose to honour both days, a decision my younger self agreed with.

But those cold, starlit nights always happened on Christmas itself. My parents began a ritual I try to keep up as well as I can. I am the oldest of seven, and so the most steeped in that ritual. Because there was always a new group of youngsters who needed their rest, my father declared that everyone would have a light lunch and we would all go to bed at four-thirty to rest until six. Then we would get up, put on our new Christmas clothes, and walk the quarter mile to my grandparents' farm.

I don't think I have ever been happier than during that brief walk. The whole family was engaged in a communal enterprise. The older children carried the younger ones or led them by their hands. My father, who rarely sang, entertained us with "Good King Wenceslas," and he pointed out the constellations, showing us the hunter Orion's Belt in the south, the Big Dipper with the Little Dipper attached to its tail in the north, and Cassiopeia, the queen, in the east. Invariably, a coyote howled from the spruces in the west.

Then suddenly we arrived at the farm with its lowing cows and the smell of new milk and hay. The house was already filled with uncles and aunts and cousins and neighbours made honorary members of the family for the day. Mugs were filled with coffee and *sukla*, Icelandic hot chocolate. The tables were loaded with food: *ponnukokurs*, Icelandic crepes filled with brown sugar; *lifrayilsa*, liver sausage; *vnarterta*, prune cake; and *skyr*, Icelandic yogurt.

Ours was not a culture that favoured discipline. Children were generally allowed to run wild, and at Christmas they were permitted to run even wilder, to eat beyond greed, and to weep and be comforted. It was a time of hugs and kisses. The children played out their little games. The women gathered to discuss family details—not gossip, because there is no need for gossip in a family where everyone knows everything, but a kind of keeping track. The men migrated to the kitchen, where my grandfather brought out a bottle of Crown Royal rye whisky and served four fingers' worth to anyone who wanted it. All of this happened under the watchful eye of the angel atop a tree covered with tinsel, icicles, and lights that bubbled.

Christmas Eve was a milder event that was shaped around the getting and receiving of presents. It preceded Christmas, of course, and it occurred at our house. The day was a flurry of activity. My father never set up the Christmas tree until the 24th, which raised the anxiety level beyond the normal fear that nothing would be ready in time.

The morning started with the opening of stockings, followed by gifts ostensibly from Santa, though most were from family members. We all wanted to know who to thank for the talking doll or the pair of hand-knit socks, and we wanted to see the look of joy of the fortunate recipients of the presents we had chosen with such care. The evening was a more intimate affair, catering to the immediate family, which nevertheless included enough uncles, aunts, and cousins to fill our medium-sized house.

I remember especially one Christmas Eve in about 1943 or so. I received a wind-up fire chief's car, a magnificent vehicle, as red as an apple and a foot long. I wound it up, and it careened across the living room floor, threatening the ankles of the entire family. Now, this was not a time in which such extravagant gifts were common, and it was clearly the best present that anyone in the family had ever seen. My father and several of his brothers immediately commandeered the car, and I didn't get to try it again until they had all put it through its paces.

I wasn't angry or upset. I knew it was my red fire chief's car, and ultimately all the relatives would have to go home and leave me alone with my car—my bright red fire chief's car, as far as I knew, the only one in the world.

The Bright Lights of Winnipeg Beach

When I was a child growing up in Gimli in the 1940s, the words "Winnipeg Beach" had all the magic of "Christmas" or "birthday." We usually went there on the 24th of May, Queen Victoria's birthday, when the entertainment opened. Perhaps we'd go back a couple of more times during the summer. The boardwalk at Winnipeg Beach was a carnival, and the circus music that played everywhere charged the air with excitement.

I had an unfortunate tendency towards motion sickness, which did nothing to dampen my enthusiasm for the rides, but considerably dampened my parents' enthusiasm for letting me go on them. If the management had known I was coming, they probably would have found some way of banning me.

Still, I remember the incredible beauty of the horses on the merry-go-round, and though I grew up on a farm and had the opportunity to ride on real horses, I preferred the stately ride of their wooden cousins.

I was always permitted to ride on the bumper cars, which, for some reason I still don't understand, allowed me to escape what in those days was always called "seasickness," no matter how you acquired it. Perhaps it was the violence of the crashes that interrupted any smooth ride, and perhaps it was my tendency to get involved in traffic gridlock with other children. At any rate, the ride was always over too soon, and in those days we were not pampered by seconds. One ride was all we got until the next time.

My father had a mild penchant for gambling, and he was particularly attracted to a game where you threw a small ball down a runway to a sort of roulette wheel, where it spun until it rested on a number that determined your prize. My father had an uncanny knack for winning boxes of chocolate, and he was often disqualified after he had won three in a row. I remember the rides home in our '37 Nash LaFayette, eating those slightly stale but still wonderful chocolates.

There were a variety of rides that spun and whirled and dipped, so that their riders were in a constant state of screaming exhilaration, but I avoided them. My brothers and sisters, on the other hand, were keen to go on them, but since my father had to accompany them, and he was even more inclined to seasickness than I was, they got to go only when older cousins happened by. Dad would gladly give up his ticket to them, as long as he didn't have to go.

The chief attraction was a terrifying roller coaster. In my memory it reached up to the lower clouds and you could see right across the lake from it. All the children told apocryphal stories about people who had been thrown from their seats and had died right there on the Winnipeg Beach grass. Once, it was rumoured, one of the cars failed

Winnipeg Beach's famous rollercaster. University of Manitoba
Archives & Special Collections, *Winnipeg Tribune* Collection PC
18/7278/18-7278-009.

Winnipeg Beach. University of Manitoba Archives & Special Collections,
Winnipeg Tribune Collection PC 18/7278/18-7278-004.

to negotiate a turn and had gone right off the tracks, killing everyone aboard.

Our parents denied these rumours, but we had the infallible authority of a kid from the city who had actually been there and seen them hauling out the bodies. When I finally got up enough nerve to try the roller coaster, I was a little older and I fell in love with it. I couldn't get enough of the slow climb to the top and the sheer horror of the trip down. When it was finally pulled down, I felt the loss deeply.

And, of course, I remember the candy apples, the spun sugar, and the ice cream cones. Winnipeg Beach days were days of free indulgence and we were denied very little. Even our mother, who believed in moderation in all things, made only token attempts to restrain us.

Winnipeg Beach was a full-time carnival in summer, as exciting at night as it was in the heat of the afternoon. They've done a lovely job of landscaping the waterfront where the boardwalk used to be, but it's not the same. Whenever I drive down the front street, I hear ghost music, and the little wooden ponies ride on into the night.

The Ice Carnival

In the 1950s and 1960s, winter carnivals dominated the lives of people in small-town Manitoba. Gimli usually held its carnival in February, but so did Winnipeg Beach, Arborg, Riverton, and every small town in Manitoba that could afford a skating rink. And whether they could afford it or not, nearly every rural Manitoba town somehow found the funds to erect a skating rink. Kids learned to skate. Province-wide tournaments allowed hockey players from Peewees to Juveniles to meet and play with their equivalents in other towns they might never otherwise have met. Lifelong friendships were made. Our coaches made contacts with North Dakota teams and parents, and American kids visited us. And we visited them back, billeting our kids at their places and going bowling, something that was fun but didn't belong to our culture at all.

The Ice Carnival was the centre of our winter celebration. The figure skaters had been practising for months for the big moment. The main event of the celebration was the choosing of the Carnival Queen. In Gimli there were always three contestants. The high school chose one young woman, the Air Force chose another, and the Chamber of Commerce chose a third. Each of the sponsoring organizations sold tickets for their contestants, and the young woman in whose name the most tickets were sold became the Carnival Queen.

The carnival was the largest fundraising initiative of the year, and the proceeds went to the skating rink. In the centre of town were billboards with thermometers painted on them. As ticket sales proceeded, the red lines that represented how much money had been taken in were regularly repainted. Volunteers selling tickets consulted these to urge their workers on to greater effort, though certain cynics argued that the winner would be the girl whose father had the deepest pockets.

The entire community took part in the preparations for the event. The rink offered figure-skating lessons for children, mostly for girls, though every so often a brave young boy would risk the taunts of his hockey-playing peers and join. As the carnival approached, the figure skaters would get out of school a half hour early in order to practise.

The carnival was also a major spectacle. The Air Force fathers provided spotlights and sound equipment and the expertise to run them. Local groups built elaborate ice castles right inside the rink. Hockey practice and games were cancelled so that the ice could be newly frozen and in perfect shape for the displays. The two-sheet curling rink next door to the skating rink became the dressing room for the skaters and the Carnival Queen contestants.

There were more than just figure skaters. Certain men took on the role of clowns and pretended that they could not skate as they did some pratfalls that must have cost them at least

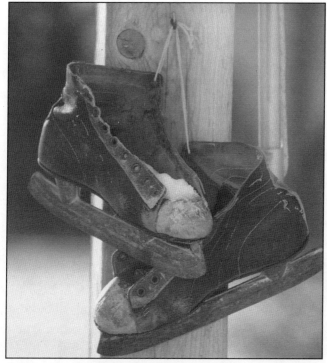

Skating never goes out of style in the Interlake. Pixabay.com, iceskates 1081852.

minor injuries. I remember one carnival in which my uncle Joe skated out and leaped over a barrel. It was replaced with an even larger barrel, which he again leaped over. Finally, they brought out a huge barrel that seemed impossible. Joe started at the end of the rink, then skated up to and through the barrel, which was made from some fragile material, and the crowd cheered wildly.

The carnival I remember most clearly took place in February 1964. My sister Judy was sponsored by the Chamber of Commerce. Her competition was Darlene Larsen, representing the RCAF, and Elinor Howart, representing the high school. The first event of the evening was the arrival of the Carnival Queen and the princesses. A Mountie in his bright red uniform led them in, the queen on his arm and the two princesses following. This was the moment we had all been waiting for. Judy entered on the Mountie's arm, signalling that she had won. They were led to an ice throne at the far end of the rink, from which they could watch the proceedings.

Then a host of tiny figure skaters appeared and danced to music from the speakers. They were followed by a local young girl who did a solo, whirled and spun, then curtseyed and left. Then another class of older girls did more complex dances. Again, the best of them did solos, all leading up to the paid, imported-from-Winnipeg, semi-professional young woman who wowed the crowd with her beauty and grace. Between the performances, the clowns entertained us all. And finally it was over and the crowd surged out onto the ice. The dancers appeared, now in street clothes. The rink was filled with congratulations and praise. Tiny girls spun in imitation of their older sisters. People in parkas and heavy winter boots danced to the music. Nobody wanted to go home.

The Best of All Possible Worlds

Ifirst learned to drive when I was six years old. The year was
1946, and the rules of farm safety were less stringent than
they are now. I was sat on the seat of an International Har-
vester Farmall tricycle tractor and showed where the steering
wheel was and how to push in the clutch and let it out on
command. We were haying along the line of spruces that ran
west for a kilometre from the farmstead. My uncles Charley
and Willie were in command. Willie was twelve and Charley was fourteen. They pointed me along the hayfield, put
the tractor into gear, and shouted commands—"Clutch in,"
"Clutch out"—while they ran like demons with their pitchforks, loading the hayrack.

It was an incredibly exuberant adventure. My brother
Gerry rode in the hayrack with Willie and begged for his
turn to drive, but it was clear that he was much too young, so
I alone commanded the Farmall, up and down the windrows,
the smell of alfalfa in my nostrils, my heart pounding and

Archives of Manitoba, New Iceland Collection 171, Friends in horse-drawn buggy, 1895, (N11183).

my sense of my own power dangerously pumping up my ego. But I was not much different from my schoolmates, who, like me, were on the cutting edge of the transition from horses to vehicles.

On the edge of the spruce bush was an old Rumely tractor, affectionally known as "Kerosene Annie" because it ran on kerosene rather than gasoline. It replaced the earlier steam tractors that helped open the West. In my community of Gimli, the Icelandic settlers referred to them as "Ketils," the Icelandic word for a kettle, and the name stuck for years, long after all tractors ran on gasoline.

I grew up on the edge of a shift from a pioneer world to a modern world. The machinery of the pioneer world ran on hay, which provided fuel for the horses and food for the cattle. Ours was a mixed farm, which meant that we raised cattle, but also sheep and pigs and chickens and foxes. (Yes, foxes. There were several fox farms near Gimli, and my father owned one. At the age of four I was bitten by a fox that I tried, unwisely, to pet.)

We cut down spruce trees into pulpwood that we hauled to a paper mill in Pine Falls, and we had our own sawmill to make lumber for the family to build garages and barns and houses. We lit our world with coal-oil lamps, and cut cordwood and split it to burn in stoves. We rose with the sun and went to bed when the sun set.

The new mechanized world was dangerous, but not much more dangerous than the disappearing world of work animals. We had an enormous bull whose only work was to breed the cattle on our farm and make short forays out into the neighbourhood to make love to the cows on somewhat poorer farms. In spite of the bull's idyllic life of indolent lovemaking, he was foul-tempered and scary. One of my chores was to take him by the ring in his nose and lead him out to the well to be watered. It was clear from his huffing and puffing that he found this a humiliating event, being led by an eight-year-old, but his humiliation was nothing compared with my daily terror of leading him.

Every day when I was six I travelled to town on the milk wagon. My cousin Dawn lived with us that year in order to attend high school, because Libau, where she and many of my cousins lived, did not offer grade twelve, which in those days was considered a serious education not available to many. But Dawn was spectacularly beautiful and equally brilliant, and she galvanized my uncles and their friends. Our trips to town were often attended by lovestruck young men eager to do anything to help. Unfortunately for them, she had an ironic sense of humour that left them tongue-tied.

Then suddenly, without anyone quite noticing or commenting on it, the modern world arrived. The horses were put out to pasture. Everything was run on gasoline. We had electric light so that we could make our own days and nights. We could buy things that we had previously had to make ourselves. Suddenly, there was a romantic world of colour movies, and then television arrived, and we could visit foreign lands in our imagination and we could dream things that had never been dreamed before.

Winter was scarier than summer, but the scariest moment of one winter was a time when my brother Gerry and I were sent out to load a hayrack and bring back the hay to the barn, where it was running low. We loaded the hayrack with our pitchforks and headed home, where lunch was waiting. We had a number of horses, Betty and Minnie, Prince and Beauty and Tom. They had all been wild horses from Saskatchewan who had to one degree or another been tamed, though only Minnie and Betty were sufficiently docile for children to deal with. My grandfather owned a dairy farm, and every day the horses pulled a wagon loaded with milk bottles to town to be delivered to customers who had no idea of the difficulty of their lives.

I told you that they were the gentlest horses on the farm. A couple of years before this, they had both come down with equine encephalitis, the sleeping sickness, and neither had ever seemed likely to rebel. But just as we headed home, a timber wolf walked out of the bush and set up a howl that I remember to this day. Betty and Minnie had other plans than becoming lunch for wolves, and they took off at a gallop. I pulled on the reins, but I might just as well have tried to pull down an old oak tree. They galloped until there was no gallop left in them.

Gerry and I clung to the hayrack, contemplating our imminent demise. But the hayrack tipped and sent us sprawling in the snow. The horses seemed to think they had done all they needed to do and started to eat the hay we had spilled. The uncles arrived and explained how it was all our fault. But they didn't send us out for hay for the rest of the winter. So I guess it all turned out for the best in this best of all possible worlds.

H.P. Tergesen's in 2017. Photo by Stefan Tergessen, used with permission.

The Stores of Gimli

The buildings of a town tell the history and culture of the community that made and used those buildings. Gimli was settled by Icelanders and Ukrainians, and the stores that they constructed help define its character. Later, Jewish and German and British settlers put their own spin on the community.

Tergesen's store on the corner of Centre and Main is the oldest building still in use. It is entering its third century, and it is impossible to think of Gimli apart from that store. It began as a two-storey building. The top storey was an unofficial town centre. Meetings and dances were held there, and for a while it served as a classroom for overcrowded schools. Later, the top storey was removed and the bottom storey was divided in two.

Two sons of the founder, HP Tergesen, shared the business. Robert Tergesen was a pharmacist, and his share of the building became a drugstore that sold prescriptions, but also had a great soda fountain and, every fall, sold the textbooks for all the schools in the area. His brother Joe turned his half of the building into a clothing store.

Later still, another generation took over, and now Stefan Tergesen runs half of the store as a high-end clothing store that has such a sense of style that people drive all the way from Winnipeg to shop there. Lorna Tergesen operates the other half as the best bookstore in rural Manitoba.

Across the street, the Lakeside Trading Company and Lumber Store was operated by the Kristjanson family and later by the Thorkelsons. It sold nearly anything you might want. I remember shopping there with my mother and father near the end of the Second World War. Harnesses hung from the walls and the ceilings, and the place was sweetly scented with the smell of leather.

Mother would bring her list and hand it to the clerk, who would gather the desired items and pack them into a box. Everywhere there were barrels and boxes with flour, raisins, dried fruit, tools, nails, horseshoes, and just about anything you might desire. Mother would tear out the beautiful coloured stamps from my ration book, which I resented deeply, and hand them to the clerk.

My father would check out the lumber that was stored in the open air behind the store, and would inevitably meet some distant friend or relative and catch up on the news. Finally, the store burned to the ground and was not replaced.

At the other end of the block, at the corner of Main and First Street North, was Greenberg's store. Like many of the stores, it was divided in two. One half was a soda fountain and restaurant with booths where you could buy sodas and milkshakes, floats and ice cream sundaes. If you were hungry you could get a hamburger and chips (the term "French fries" may have been used elsewhere, but it didn't come to Gimli until later).

The other half of the store was a grocery. What I remember about it mostly was its array of fresh and dried fruit. Bananas hung from the ceiling, their ends attached so that they hung upward, or so it seemed to me. If you needed bananas the owner, Jake Greenberg, or his son Harry would climb up a stepladder and hack off the fruit with a machete. Oddly, the grocery sold cans of tobacco and bullets for twenty-two rifles.

The other store in Gimli that sold Jewish food was the Breeze Inn. It was originally opened by the Stefanson family. It operated only in the summer, but it sold kosher meat and great sandwiches, along with incredibly cold soft drinks.

There were a lot of Ukrainian stores where the main language of commerce was Ukrainian. The K&K store operated by Adam Kasupski was on Main Street opposite to Greenberg's where the library now is. Mike Shewaga operated a convenience store in South Beach opposite to where Gimli Lumber used to be. He sold to Stan Kurlicki, who added an ice house and delivered ice to campers and residents who had iceboxes, the ancestors of refrigerators. His competition was Mike Evans, who operated a small store very near to Stan's and who was reputed to have the best ice cream in town.

Meanwhile, Mike Shewaga took his profit from his sale to Stan Kurlicki and moved to the north end on Park Road, where he opened on the corner of Highway 9. Skomeroskis had their own store on the corner of Highway 9 and 5th Street North.

The Kressock family opened a store on the corner of Highway 9. They operated it for several years, then sold out to the Rudney family. After the Rudneys left, it morphed into a series of restaurants and has now turned into Mask restaurant.

A classic Gimli store was known only as Slobodian's or "the second-hand store." It was kitty-corner to where the Credit Union now stands. Two Icelandic men, the Kristjanson brothers, Hannes and Ted, married the Slobodian daughters Anne and Sophie. After Mr. Slobodian the elder died, the sisters ran the operation and renamed it the Target store.

Like the citizens of a town, the stores that support it grow and fade. They have their moments of glory, and though most of the stores I have mentioned are gone now, their ghosts live on in the memories of Gimli dwellers.

Archives of Manitoba, New Iceland Collection 201, H.P. Tergesen store, Gimli, [ca. 1915], (N11212).

New Iceland as a Literary Landscape

New Iceland is a historic geographical and political enti-
ty, a place on the west shore of Lake Winnipeg that was
precisely measured and named. It is also the site of a discourse
about the Icelanders who left their home country to settle in
America. It is an imaginative site, a place filled with dramatic
action including floods, locusts, a smallpox epidemic, a religious controversy, and a political struggle. Historians, political scientists, legal experts, writers, and filmmakers have
represented New Iceland in a variety of conflicting ways. The
precise boundaries both in space and time are in dispute. The
evidence is unclear. Even eyewitness descriptions of the same
event are often completely different.

Any town, city, country, or settlement is at least as much
a product of human imagination as it is a physical space. We
understand the idea of place as the product of representation.
There are, of course, many different forms of representation.
A place may be represented through drawings, painting, or

photographs. It may be represented through music or dance or any number of different ways of responding, but the main way in which places are represented is through writing.

New Iceland is a concept more than a place. It existed from 1875 until 1887 as the Icelandic Reserve, created by a series of Orders-in-Council from the Canadian Federal Government. It had a constitution, a set of laws, and a government based on the old Icelandic government system, though the constitution and the laws were never officially recognized by the Canadian government.

Still, whatever the legalities, New Iceland continued to be a sort of floating signifier to refer to the area along the shore of Lake Winnipeg where the Icelandic settlers had arrived in 1875, but also to refer to a particular culture and its aspirations. The idea behind New Iceland was that it would be a continuation of Icelandic language and culture in a new location in the New World.

New Iceland continues to exist as a site of a discourse about the historic diaspora of Icelanders in the New World. It exists in the form of poetry, fiction, letters, memoirs, scholarly analysis, historical descriptions, legal documents, songs, and plays. Much of the history of the place is in dispute, and eyewitness accounts of certain key events are radically different.

Any attempt to reconstruct historical cultures and events is forever contaminated by self-interest and by ideology. Anthropologists use the artifacts they uncover to reinforce notions of national destiny, or to help justify hegemony over other cultures. In a similar way cultural archaeology as it is practised in representing New Iceland is contaminated by ideology and self-interest.

The relationship to the mother country is also problematic. Many of the casual poems published in the early years of the settlement are like the poems of yearning by other immigrants to Canada. They yearn for the mountains and valleys and rivers of the home place. But the Icelandic Canadian newspaper *Framfari* published a poem by a writer listed only as BS, entitled "Farewell to Iceland from One Leaving for America." The poem appeared on April 5, 1878. In it the poet lists the reasons he does not love Iceland.

"I love you little or not at all," the poet writes, "you grassless land of Icelandic sulphur." He goes on to detail the things he does not love:

I have no love for Hekla and the blue peaks
nor for the high, bald summits of the glaciers,
for they give off dark mists
and cold fog which would sweep over everyone.
I have no love for the brownish rivers here
mixed with glacial gravel,
nor for the evil-smelling creek
that has often been noxious to men.
Nor do I love the blizzards and storms that rage here,
nor the ice from Greenland's coasts,
nor the dusty places, the desert land
where through the ages all has been covered with sand.

A gentler farewell to Iceland was written by Helga Steinunn Baldvinsdóttir, who wrote under the name Undina:

The trusty vessel must convey
a pallid maiden on waves

frosty island of ice away
out on the blue ocean way

Now on a wave of salty sea
the sun it does descend
just as the gentle tears proceed
which from a mournful eye fall free

Gone is the peak, gone is the farm
gone so abruptly the valley
gone is the spring, so crystal-clear
gone the beloved, far and near

Farewell to a woman and hearty man
farewell to the grove in flower
farewell to my truly cherished land
farewell to the times now passed at hand

The initial settlement was something of a disaster. A hand-ful of Icelanders had arrived in 1873 and settled in Wisconsin. The main body of Icelanders, however, arrived in Kinmount, Ontario. After a year they sent an expedition to Manitoba in search of a site where they could construct a new Iceland. They arrived at the site late in the year without proper equip-ment and supplies, and suffered through a fierce winter and the onset of a smallpox epidemic.

Still, within little more than a year they had established a newspaper, *Framfari*, and begun a series of debates about the future of the colony. The colony was remarkably literary. Almost everyone wrote poetry, though much of it was not remarkable for its quality. Vidar Hreinsson, who has studied the early poetry, wrote in a 1993 article in *Scandinavian-Canadian Studies*:

> The poetry that directly deals with the emigration, either the departure, the motherland or the new world is monotonous. Many poems express sorrow over the departure. Soon a certain self-representation was developed, repeated again and again, in parts or as a whole: Icelandic nature and history is glorified, its present state lamented, the emigrants view themselves as seeking freedom, parallel to the settlers of Iceland and the Vinland explorers.

Kristjana Gunnars, in her *Settlement Poems* (1980), tries to recreate a feeling of the early settlement. She studied Iceland folklore at the University of Iceland, specializing in the folk magic and medicine of the period shortly before the settlers left for Canada. She reasoned that just because the immigrants left Iceland, they would not leave behind the folk wisdom that informed their culture. That folk wisdom, however, was rooted in Icelandic geography, climate, and culture, and it would fail to work in Canada. The settlers would have to come to grips with the new land, and that might often be harsh and violent.

Settlement Poems begins with an invocation of folk wisdom that is gentle and domestic:

to stay together: don't air your quilt
on Sundays, don't give each other
a sharp tool

eat the heart of ptarmigan
put two tongues under your tongue & kiss

hang a raven's heart around your neck
hang a crow's heart around your neck

By the end of Book 1, the new land has taught a different
kind of folk wisdom:

open the cut at the breast bone
back to the vent
through the abdomen, slip
the edge of the scalpel under

the skin, wall opens with a shot
of knife, intestine juices run
sprinkle sawdust on the flesh
to catch, dry

this stomach reads well
defines
the sustenance of a new land

Here there is a more violent way of understanding the
nature of a new land.

Perhaps the best evocation of New Iceland and the Icelandic experience in the New World is Laura Goodman Salverson's *The Viking Heart* (1923). The story begins in Iceland
with a romantic evocation of a peaceful and beautiful land
where Einar Halsson and his family reside: "At the edge of
the world the sun had dipped his glowing face in a jade sea
and the summer twilight had descended—the wonderful
twilight of a land of the midnight sun! Hill and dale and valley were wrapped in trailing shadows, light airy shadows like

the veils of a thousand elves." In that moment of peace, the son of the family, Carl, yearns to travel to America. "The old restlessness of the ancient Norsemen—a longing for the new and strange—a desire that has never wholly left their descendants, was awake in his young veins."

Moments later they face complete disaster. A volcano has exploded and its lava sweeps everything the family owns, and including Carl, into the sea. The father and mother and daughter make it to a boat, but the Iceland they have known has completely disappeared. By the second chapter they have arrived at Fisher's Landing, North Dakota, on their way to New Iceland.

Salverson begins to eulogize the Icelanders and their spirit. "But the Icelander is not of peasant ancestry," she tells us. "He is not an agriculturist by instinct or inclination, nor is he a creature all brawn who may labor from sunrise to sunset without those pangs which are the penalty of intelligence."

As they travel towards New Iceland, they encounter their first Indigenous man: "there flashed into sight from beyond a bend in the river a craft, long and slender, cleaving the water with the swiftness and silence of thought. And the foreigners from the far north country saw their first red man. A splendid native, straight and supple, like some bronzed god baring his copper chest indifferent to the elements." It is the first but by no means the last evocation of a strong relationship between the Indigenous peoples and the Icelanders. There is as well the story of John Ramsay, the Indigenous man who has lost his land to the Icelanders, but who nevertheless remains a good friend to them.

The Halssons are soon all dead, felled by the smallpox epidemic, except for the daughter Borga, who encounters Bjorn

Lindal and marries him, and their family becomes the focus
of the story. Bjorn and Borga give birth to Thor, a young man
who exemplifies all the Viking virtues. When the Great War
comes along, he enlists, and his mother and her friend Finna
go to watch them march by.

They are both fascinated. "The centuries are long since
the sons of Iceland lived by war. It takes much sometimes to
rekindle the old desires. But it is doubtful whether there will
not always lie buried in the Icelandic heart a certain dangerous fire—just as the icebound mountains of his country hide,
however deep, their deadly flames."

The military procession finally brings Borga to accept her
new nationality: "For the first time in her life she thought
of Canada as a dear and precious possession—these soldiers
had somehow made it so… They were hers, somehow, these
marching men. They might have been an army of ancient
Norsemen, so dear they seemed." The taking of the New
World requires a sacrifice, and that sacrifice is Thor, who dies
at the end of the novel and by so doing makes the New Icelanders into Canadians.

The Viking Heart suggests a special spirit that moves the
Icelandic immigrants, a spirit that derives from the Vikings
and the early Norsemen, and is found in the great literature
of the sagas. Many of the historians who have dealt with New
Iceland seem to have tacitly accepted this position, and their
tales are usually about the heroic overcoming of hardship.

The final creation of an image of New Iceland is not a
piece of writing at all, but a film, *Tales from the Gimli Hospital,* which writer and director Guy Maddin originally wanted
to call *The Gimli Saga.* The film is a black and white story
in which a grandmother in the Gimli hospital tells a series

of stories to her grandchildren. The stories are a wonderful mishmash of New Iceland history, in which various episodes are mixed up and the figure of John Ramsay inhabits the story like a ghost. At the comedic centre of the story is an incident in which an Icelandic man rubs his hair with a fish in an attempt to make himself more beautiful. It's the sort of a story that a fifteen-year-old boy who had heard only fragments of the story of the settlement might have believed, but Guy Maddin took it seriously, and the film is brilliant, both as a gothic tale and a warning to Icelanders not to take themselves too seriously. The media assumed that the people of Gimli would be mightily offended by the film, but I was there when it was first shown, and almost everyone I know was a bit bewildered but thoroughly entertained.

Gimli's viking statue.

Laxness in Manitoba

The Nobel Prize-winning Icelandic writer Halldor Laxness died recently in his mid-nineties. Though it would
be going too far to call him a Manitoba writer, he did live for
a while in Manitoba, and he wrote a short story while he was
here. The reaction of the local Icelandic community to that
story was one of the reasons he went back to Iceland.

I met Laxness in 1983. I had been invited to do a reading at the University of Iceland, and the novelist Sigurdur A.
Magnusson, who was then the head of the Icelandic Writer's
Union, was my host. I wanted to meet Laxness, but by that
time he had stopped giving audiences. Magnusson said he'd
see what he could do.

The next day he told me that Laxness had agreed to meet
me, but a photographer from *People* magazine would be
photographing Laxness for an article they were planning to
do about him. That was fine with me, and we set out that
afternoon for Laxness's house. It was my first encounter with

Icelandic drivers, and while Magnusson was no more reckless than anyone else on the road, it was a little like taking part in the Indy 500.

Laxness turned out to be a small, almost elfin man with restless energy and a sharp wit. The photographer was a Russian émigré from Paris, who spoke French but neither Icelandic nor English. Laxness spoke to him in French so execrable that I was willing to use my own meagre resources. "If you want to speak a language, just speak it," Laxness told me. "Don't worry about getting it correct. The point is communication, not elegance." And with that, he broke into Russian, for which the photographer seemed grateful. It turned out that Laxness could use dozens of languages at various levels, so he wasn't quite sure how many languages he spoke.

The photographer began shooting pictures with his motorized cameras, circling around to get different angles. In the next two hours he shot thirty-eight rolls of thirty-six pictures each. Laxness paid no more attention to him than if he were a butterfly in a garden. Instead, he ran to his study to bring out a copy of the latest translation of his novel *Independent People*. It had been translated into over one hundred different languages, he said. This latest version was in Swahili.

Independent People is one of my favourite novels, and I told him so. The main character, Bjartur of Summerhouses, is so recklessly individualistic that he destroys almost everything he loves. His daughter, Asta Sollilja, the beautiful girl with the squint eye, is heartbreakingly vulnerable.

Laxness wasn't surprised. "Everybody loves it," he said, not bragging, simply as a fact. He told me that if you counted all the different languages into which it has been translated, it was the best-selling novel in history. Perhaps my memory plays me false, but I think I remember his claiming it had sold twenty-five million copies in China and thirteen million in Russia. I do know that Shrinivas Pradhan, who did his PhD in English at the University of Manitoba, told me that he had heard Laxness speak in India and read the novel, and it had changed his life.

Laxness was more interested in talking to me about his stay in Manitoba. At the time, he had just begun his writing career and was considering moving to Canada. The first great rush to the New World from Iceland was over by then, but Laxness thought he would at least check New Iceland out.

He spent several months in Manitoba, and he published a short story while he was here. The characters in the story were Canadian Icelanders, and Laxness did not present them in the noblest light. It was a realist story, he explained, and the characters had the normal flaws of human beings.

Apparently, the local Icelanders were not keen on having their flaws, normal or not, paraded before the world. Laxness had been invited to a party before the story was published, but it had come out by the date of the party. He was a young writer then, and anxious that people like his work. His host welcomed him in and offered him a cup of coffee. Nobody else at the party would speak to him at all. He spent the evening alone on the porch, he said, listening to people in the other room talk about what a horrible thing he had done to present the community in such a terrible light. That night helped him make his decision. He would go back to Iceland to do his writing. There is a rumour that the community was about to tar and feather him, but Laxness himself knew nothing of that.

And so we lost a Nobel Prize-winning writer. Or maybe

he would never have written *Independent People* if he had stayed. It's hard to know.

Laxness left the room and returned moments later in his bathing suit. This was a signal that the interview and the photography session were over. We walked out with him to the swimming pool beside his house. The pool was constantly replenished by the water from a hot spring on the mountainside above the house. The mist from the hot pool in the cool early June evening made us all into ghostly figures. Laxness plunged into the pool and that was the last I saw of him until about six months later, when his picture appeared in *People* magazine. He looks almost Russian in the photo.

Skrag: A Dog of the World

I grew up in the country surrounded by animals, wild and tame, and sometimes even halfway between wild and tame. At one time we had sixteen cats and twelve dogs. I soon learned that every one of them had its own personality, its own likes and dislikes. We had two three-legged cats and one three-legged dog. On several occasions people from the city dropped off pregnant dogs at the edge of the bush. Somehow, the animals found my mother, who fed them and petted them. Three different times a mother dog with many pups arrived from the bush and delivered her progeny to Mother, who fed and tamed the little ones and found them good homes.

I was thinking about the various dogs of my childhood and decided to write a long poem about a dog who would be a combination of all the dogs I have known. I asked poet Dennis Cooley what he thought I should name the dog. He thought for a moment and told me "Skrag." And at that instant Skrag came into existence.

There's a little bit of Skrag in every farm dog. Photo by Rob Gordon, used with permission.

From the very first word I wrote, the dog became a heroic and epic creature, filled with love and lust. He was part animal, part philosopher. The farm where I had spent much of my youth became the country that Skrag ruled and from which he dispensed wisdom and advice.

The poem ended suddenly before I knew what was happening. I typed to the end of a line and discovered that Skrag had died, killed by the narrator of my poem. I sent the poem off to *Grain* magazine, where the editors published it, asking only that I bring him back to life by omitting the final section in which he dies tragically. I agreed, and it came out in that form.

I tried to keep the poem going, but I could not. Nothing came into my imagination. And I learned that when your dog is dead, your dog is dead. Fictional resurrection is as difficult as real resurrection and equally unlikely. The next time I published the poem, I reverted to the original version.

My fictional dog took his place among a vast list of fictional animals that inhabit our literature, from White Fang and Lassie to Moby Dick and My Friend Flicka. The moment you begin to try to enumerate fictional animals, you are overwhelmed by sheer numbers. When I was young, fictional creatures inhabited books, and a few apparently lived in the radio. Now, with the proliferation of media, films, television, online music, children's theatre, and recordings, imaginary animals are everywhere.

I am interested here in animals that had a real life before I fictionalized them, animals that were grounded in the actual world. My grandfather's dog, Sport, was a large black, brown, and white dog who appeared to have gathered up some German Shepherd DNA, though, unlike actual shepherds, he was completely resistant to training. He had, however, an anarchic spirit that I used in my fictional Skrag.

What I learned by growing up on a farm was that animals are not very different from us. They suffer like we do from illness. They can become sad. They can feel love and they can be quietly happy. Once, and this is a story told me by my grandmother, the horse Betty gave birth to a foal that was frail and kept the barn upset by its mournful bleating. They were separated in hopes that they would settle down.

The next morning, the foal had died in its stall, as often happened to farm animals. Betty was insane with what we could only call grief. When they harnessed Betty and tried to make her drag her foal to the manure pile where dead animals were taken, Betty turned over the sled with her foal's body and ran for an entire mile before anyone could catch her. From then on, she would not go near the site of her dead foal, and no one dared to try to make her.

Life on the farm is a microcosm of the wide world. Creatures are born and die every day. There isn't much room for sentiment. But it is impossible to represent the world in story or song without sentiment. I might be accused of anthropomorphizing the animals by giving them human characteristics. But anyone who has grown up on a farm will know that animals have feelings just as we do, and it is no sin to give them their due. They make our lives better just by being alive, and they deserve to have their dignity.

The Sporting Life

People who grew up in Gimli had sports at the centre of their winter lives. I grew up on a farm south of the town. I learned to skate on a slough just east of our house. My first skates, handed down to me from one of my many uncles, had two blades for each skate, like something out of the novel *Hans Brinker, or The Silver Skates*. My father shovelled the snow off the little pond behind our house and my mother brought out an old wooden chair to be my first dancing partner. I leaned on the chair and pushed it around the pond. It was fiercely cold but I don't think I ever had more fun than on that day.

Later, I got real skates and went to the rink in town to practise. I was never a great skater because we lived in the country and I could go to skate only when there was someone to drive me. I joined the Peewee hockey squad, and thus began what turned out to be a truncated career as a hockey star. We played inter-squad games and sometimes we played a team from Arborg or Riverton. I graduated to the Bantam B team and got to travel even farther afield. Somehow we made it to the provincial finals, largely through the talents of Walter Einarson, who many years later has given up hockey to sell Fords.

My one chance of real glory came in the final game against Roland-Miami. The score was tied. I found myself alone at the red line when the puck came right to my stick. There was no one between me and the goalie, who had turned around to talk to the goal judge and who didn't see me coming. I took careful aim and raised the puck over the goal, the goalie, and the goal judge, and up into the third balcony. The place erupted in applause, but not because of my skill. A couple of minutes later the enemy scored, and even Walter Einarson's undeniable skill was not enough to save us.

I persevered for a while and joined the Juvenile team, but the coach decided that because of my large size, I should move to defence. I lasted about a month and then I switched to curling, where I was not expected to body-check anyone.

Actually, I turned out to be a pretty good curler. All the high school teams were required to have at least one girl. My team was composed of me, Marie Scribner, who had half the boys in school in love with her, Keith Gottfried, who had half the girls in school in love with him, and Lesley Stoodley, who had just arrived from Newfoundland and had never thrown a rock in his life. We didn't lose a game that season, partly because of skill but also because of the distraction factor that Marie and Keith provided.

Like most Manitobans I took the game of curling as an integral part of my life. I curled in the Manitoba School Bonspiel, then at university, and later as a member of a dozen different senior and mixed teams. I won all sorts of prizes in those bonspiels, not many things that I wanted or needed, but trophies all the same.

I loved the camaraderie of the sport, the fact that after every game you shook hands with each member of the opposing team. There was no anger, no rancour, and even the competitiveness was gentle. I curled in the annual Guys and Dolls Bonspiel and the Winnipeg Bonspiel, which, when I curled in it, was the biggest in the world.

Then the Braunstein brothers and their team took curling another step. They played like professionals, practising like no one had done before. They introduced new strategies and a whole new way of sliding. They wiped out every team in Manitoba and pretty much every team in the country. They were gentlemanly and good-humoured, but they changed curling forever. Local leagues still play the old game, but you cannot play in the big leagues unless you are professional.

I'd probably still be curling if arthritis had not taken me out of contention. I loved and still love the game. I loved the camaraderie, the social life, the tension of the competition, the fact that it was and is intensely a team sport. It was and it still is a community-builder.

But I must point out that every generation has its own heroes, its own iconic figures who are larger than life and who shape the imaginations of the young. I grew up first idolizing the boxers my father and his brothers followed on radio. There were two boxers who captured the spirit of the age. They were Joe Louis and Jersey Joe Walcott.

Radio became a powerful force for the dissemination of sporting events. Radios became affordable in the 1920s, but it was not until 1936 that the CBC came into existence and started to broadcast sporting events nationally. Boxing became immensely popular because throughout most of Canada there was little chance of actually seeing a boxing match. My father and his brothers bought two pairs of boxing gloves and they and their friends spent their Sunday afternoons taking part in amateur matches. And whenever there was a serious match, they huddled around the radio, cheering on their favourites, though in my family Joe Louis was always the favourite.

The same thing happened a little later with hockey. The entire country divided itself into Toronto Maple Leafs fans and Montreal Canadiens fans. I became a Leafs fan, not because that was a rational decision when I was three years old, but because my babysitter, Bernice, was a Leafs fan who insisted on absolute silence during the games. And, of course, the greatest of all players was Teeder Kennedy. Bernice did admit that there was something to be said for Rocket Richard, though she cursed him roundly when he appeared on *Hockey Night in Canada*.

Gimli had one sport that was not shared with the rest of the country. That sport was Icelandic *Glima* wrestling. Two men faced each other wearing harnesses that went around the waist and one leg. The contestants grabbed each other's harness and tried to throw the opponent off balance and onto the ground. It required considerable strength, balance, and timing, and resembled a kind of restrictive judo.

Feats of strength were a part of Icelandic culture, and the Icelandic settlers brought their passion for lifting things to Canada. I have an old black and white photograph that is now badly tattered, but it shows my father with a rope that went around his neck to the engine of a 1929 Dodge. He has lifted the engine off the ground, no small feat on its own, but in this case there are two men standing on the engine. Really.

Dogs were everywhere, and so of course they took part in the sporting life. In the early days, sleigh dogs were beasts of burden. They hauled the fishermen out to their nets and they hauled the catch back to towns around Lake Winnipeg. But wherever there is a chance to turn work into play, humans will take that chance. Soon after the first settlement of the area, dog-team races became an important winter sport.

My great-grandfather, Captain Baldi Anderson, had an excellent racing team of huskies, and he won several races. During the winter he brought his team to Winnipeg and made a living offering Winnipeggers rides around Central Park at twenty-five cents a ride. He was also involved as an official, and took part in the International Winnipeg to Minneapolis Five Hundred Mile Race. That race is commemorated in Carl Sandburg's poem "Manitoba Childe Roland," a parody of Robert Browning's "Childe Roland To The Dark Tower Came."

The Manitoba version tells the story of a six-year-old girl who is read a heroic story about the race:

I flash to the form of a man to his hips in snow drifts
of Manitoba and Minnesota—in the sled derby run
from Winnipeg to Minneapolis.

He is beaten in the race the first day out of Winnipeg—
the lead dog is eaten by four team mates—and the
man goes on and on—running while the other racers
ride, running while the other racers sleep—

Lost in a blizzard twenty-four hours, repeating a circle
of travel hour after hour—fighting the dogs who
dig holes in the snow and whimper for sleep—
pushing on—running and walking five hundred
miles to the end of the race—

Just before the outbreak of the First World War, the idea
of Antarctic exploration became very popular. Scott and
Amundsen's race to be first to the South Pole stirred the
blood of every young man looking for adventures, and there
were many of them. Ernest Shackleton's attempt to cross the
Antarctic received far more volunteers than could be accom-
modated, and a myth developed about the expedition. Shackleton is supposed to have placed an ad that read:

MEN WANTED: FOR HAZARDOUS JOUR-
NEY. SMALL WAGES, BITTER COLD, LONG
MONTHS OF COMPLETE DARKNESS, CON-
STANT DANGER, SAFE RETURN DOUBTFUL.
HONOUR AND RECOGNITION IN CASE OF
SUCCESS.

—SIR ERNEST SHACKLETON

Apparently the desire for romantic adventure reached all
the way to Lake Winnipeg. Everyone in the area has a story
of some relative or neighbour who applied but somehow
missed the journey. It was the quality of our sled dogs, it was
rumoured, that made Shackleton aim his ad at us particularly.

No copy of the advertisement has ever been found, but just think of the glory that nearly touched our town.

Curling has its own anthem, John K. Samson's song "Tournament of Hearts." John is an internationally famous singer and songwriter. He is deeply interested in community and in his local place. And he is a curler. He and Christine Fellows, his wife and fellow singer, took part in the 112th Annual International Bonspiel at the Dawson Curling Club. And his album with his band The Weakerthans, *Reconstruction Site,* relates an imagined conversation between one of Shackleton's men and the philosopher Michel Foucault.

Sled dog racing has a long and proud history in Manitoba. Long before there were any white folk in Manitoba, Indigenous tribes owned working dogs and almost certainly used them for sport. Now, sled dog racing has largely been replaced by snowmobile racing. The area around Gimli has extensive groomed trails suitable for racing snowmobiles, and outdoor parties and picnics are popular.

Automobile racing on Lake Winnipeg in winter has developed over the past years. It began with races on the ice just out from the Gimli pier. The most popular cars were Austin Minis and small foreign cars. Lately, the sport has developed rapidly, and in the winter of 2017 Mercedes-Benz offered a crash course in ice racing as part of its AMG Winter Sporting program. The Winnipeg Sports Car Club has been active in sport racing in Gimli since 1952 and now coordinates ice racing at the Gimli Ice Carnival.

We are a northern people with long, cold winters. We make our fun in many ways, from cross-country skiing, tobogganing, and snowshoeing to skating, ice fishing, and ice sailing. Given our weather, it would be madness to do anything else.

Archives of Manitoba, New Iceland Collection 295, Pioneers playing croquet, [ca. 1910], (N11299).

Archives of Manitoba, New Iceland Collection 264, Tug-of-war at Icelandic Celebration Day in Gimli, 2 August 1912, (N11268).

Summer Sports

The Icelandic Celebration was held in Winnipeg from 1890 to 1932, after which it took place in Gimli. From its inception, sports were an important part of the occasion. Wilhelm Kristjanson, in his *The Icelandic People in Manitoba: A Manitoba Saga* (1965), wrote:

> Formerly, the sports events were a prominent feature of the day, and for many years the program included, besides track and field events, Icelandic wrestling, middle distance running, bicycle racing, archery, and baseball. Athletic clubs from Winnipeg, Selkirk, Lundar, Argyle and Gimli, and individuals from other places competed and a high standard was set in the period from 1905 to 1940 by such outstanding athletes as Kristjan Backman, Magnus Kelly, the brothers Jack and Ben Baldwin, Einar Johnson, Bjorgvin Stefansson, AO (Gusti) Magnusson, Sveinn Sigfusson and others. The

coveted trophies were the Oddson Shield for Club competitions and the Hanson Cup for individual championship.

The 1950 Islendingadagurinn program set out the rules for the Oddson Shield and Hanson Cup competitions. The Oddson Shield would be held for one year by the winning club. The Hanson Cup would be held for one year by the aggregate winner of individual events, where first place was worth three points, second was worth two points, and third was worth one point. The closed events for the Oddson Shield and the Hanson Cup included the 100-yard dash; the running broad jump; the 440-yard race; the high jump; the 220-yard race; the hop, step, and jump; the shot put; the 880-yard race; and the one-mile race. In addition, there were four open events, including a 100-yard dash, an 880-yard race, a running broad jump, and a pole vault. Four or more contestants were required to compete in each event, and all competitors competed at their own risk.

The Oddson Shield was presented to the Icelandic Celebration Committee by Thorsteinn Oddson and Sons in 1913 for annual competition among track and field clubs representing the Icelandic community. It is a magnificent trophy and includes the names of the winning clubs from 1913 to 1941. The most consistent winner of the trophy was the Grettir Amateur Athletic Association of Lundar, who held the shield for ten consecutive years from 1914 to 1923, and won it fifteen times in all. The AGGHR Club (Arborg, Gimli, Geysir, Hnausa, and Riverton) won it three times in 1939, 1940, and 1941. Other winners included the Viking AAC and the Falcon AAC from Winnipeg, the Gimli Athletic Club, Sleipnir, and Einmannafelag. The competitions were revived in 1950 when the shield was won by the Manitoba Settlers, and were held sporadically until 1969. The Winnipeg Flying M Club won it in 1959, 1960, and 1961.

The Hanson Cup for individual performance was given to the Icelandic Celebration Committee in 1913. It replaced the Clemens, Arnason, Palmason trophy that had been won permanently by Einar Johnson of Oak Point, a member of the Grettir Amateur Athletic Association. The Hanson Cup is to be kept by the committee and a miniature trophy given to the winner.

The 1970 program thanks the Canadian Track and Field Association for sanctioning the Western Canadian Ten Mile Championship Road Race, and the Manitoba Track and Field Association, who also endorsed the race. The race has been run every year since 1970. Its most frequent winner is Chris McCubbins of Winnipeg.

In addition to the Oddson Shield and the Hanson Cup, six additional trophies were offered in 1970. They included the Svein Sigfusson Trophy for Highest Point Standings in Men's Midget and Juvenile Events, the Einar B. Johnson Trophy for the Highest Point Standings in Men's Open Track Events, the Jan Maddin Trophy for the highest point standings in Women's Open Events, the Dr. Alsi E. Thorlakson Wengek Trophy for Highest Point Standings in Women's Midget and Juvenile Events, the Icelandic Canadian Club Trophy for the Winner of the 10 Mile Road Race, and the Steward Trophy for the Winner of the Juvenile 10 Mile Road Race.

When I began to take part in the sports programs in the late fifties and early sixties, the glory days were over. There were only four or five of us in each event, so winning a ribbon was no great feat. The prize money was five dollars for first place, three dollars for second, and a dollar for third. Still, a ribbon is a ribbon, and we wore them as proudly as if they were Olympic medals.

As time passed, it became increasingly difficult to maintain organized sports. There were many reasons for this. The park at Gimli did not have the kind of track needed for formal athletic competitions. As long as the competitions were tied to the Icelandic Celebration in Gimli, there was little chance of the competitions' gaining wide recognition. When the events remained loosely structured and fully amateur, there was an audience for the events and enough participants to run them. As provincial sports organizations came into existence, interest in amateur sports dwindled. There have been attempts to restore sports to their ancient glory, such as the McMahon Mile, but most of these have survived for only a short time.

The sports that have survived are those that invite large-scale participation and that downplay expertise. The children's races are always popular, as are the comic sports such as the Grandma Gallop, open only to grandmothers, the sack races, the wheelbarrow races, and the egg-and-spoon races. The Father and Daughter Three-Legged Race and its companion, the Mother and Son Race, are the highlights. It is debatable whether the sandcastle-building competition constitutes an actual sport, but it is very popular, and its winners are celebrated as passionately as in more athletic contests.

Gimli has its own sports not performed in many places. The Islendingadunk, a sport reputedly imported from Iceland, uses a large pole that has been greased and secured to the dock so that it is over the water. Contestants dressed in life vests sit on the pole, facing each other. Each contestant has a large sack filled with some floatable material. The contestants swing their sacks at the opponents in an attempt to knock them into the water. It doesn't seem a game of skill, but often the same people win year after year.

The other main local game is Fris-Nok. It was invented about thirty years ago by local expert Cameron Arnason. The game is played by erecting two two-by-fours about ten metres apart. Teams of two players stand behind the posts, one player from each team taking turns to try to throw a Frisbee to knock the opposing team's bottle from the post. If the bottle (usually a beer bottle) hits the ground, the throwers score a point. If the bottle and Frisbee are both caught, the point is saved. Formal championships are held each year at the celebration weekend. But the game is so popular that home courts are built throughout the district. There are even rumours of a tournament that was held in Australia, and we are hoping for recognition by the International Olympic Committee.

Delicious saskatoons. Wikimedia Commons *Amelanchier alnifolia* 2802.

Berry Picking in Gimli

I come from a berry-picking family. Some of my earliest memories are of accompanying my grandmother and my mother on expeditions into the bush around Gimli to pick wild strawberries and raspberries, wild plums, black currants, saskatoons, chokecherries, pin cherries, and cranberries. When I was young almost everyone picked berries and made either jams and jellies or preserves. Most people knew where the best berries grew, and we'd often meet other pickers from the area, and so berry picking, though a competitive enterprise, was also a social event.

The area around Gimli is remarkably endowed with wild berries. My mother's favourite were saskatoons, which she preserved as a dessert in quart jars. She stored these in the basement on shelves along with her green tomato pickles and a variety of jellies and jams. As our family increased in size, we collected more and more berries, and our mother's workload increased. There were seven of us children, but only four of us became fanatics, organizing expeditions right to the present.

In the early days we were limited to the bushes and fields within walking distance. Then, when I, the oldest, got a driver's licence and a car, the whole municipality was at our mercy. Every spring we would drive the back roads, looking for the flowering shrubs. We learned to identify the bushes by their leaves and we made maps of their location for each other. We discovered wild asparagus and marked the plants with red ribbons so that we could find them the following spring.

Berry bushes tend to grow along the edges of other bushes so that the sun strikes them from the south or the west. They ripen at different times. Wild strawberries are in the fields by mid-June. Raspberries are about a month later. Ripening time is affected by cold or warm springs and by late frosts. Saskatoons usually ripen about mid-July, but the weather can advance or retard the season by a couple of weeks. Choke-cherries and pin cherries are ready in early to mid-August. The last to ripen are cranberries. They should be picked when the berries are yellow turning to red. At that stage they have enough pectin to jell with a simple boiling and with-out added Certo. Black currants are the most difficult. They ripen unevenly, and a single shrub may have both under-ripe and overripe berries. Besides this, they have a stem and a residual flower so that each berry must be cleaned twice. Sand cherries grow along the beaches near Gimli. They are the only true cherry native to Manitoba. They produce large, black cherries that are sour to eat but make wonderful jelly.

When we pick berries, we use ice cream pails tied with small ropes so that the pail hangs on the chest. This leaves both hands free, one for holding the branches and the other for picking the berries. It is best to have a couple of extra pails, because you will often find two or three kinds of berries ripe.

Once the berries are picked, they must be cleaned before they are boiled. You can clean by hand, but there are shortcuts that can help with this tedious chore. You can take a piece of plywood and nail a couple of boards to it in the shape of a V. Incline the plywood slightly and let the berries roll down towards the narrow point of the V. The perfect berries will roll easily, but those that are misshapen or have been attacked by insects will not roll. Next, take the good berries and put them in a pail. Set up a fairly strong fan and pour the berries through the breeze into another pail. This will blow away all the leaves, twigs, and dust, leaving the berries ready for their final wash in cold water. When they are clean, cover with water to the level of the berries and boil. Filter the juice through cheesecloth or an old but clean pillow cover, hang, and let the juice drip overnight. Don't squeeze, or you will not get clear jelly.

My second passion beyond berry picking and canning is growing and collecting herbs. Each year I grow about sixty different kinds of herbs and collect others that grow wild. Not many people know that wild caraway grows along the edges of most of the roads in the municipality, or that rosehips make both wonderful jelly and wonderful wine.

Almost every herb figures in mythology. Herbs touch the human body in several ways. Some have medicinal qualities, such as feverfew and comfrey. Others make fine perfumes and sachets. Still others are aids to beauty. But it is the culinary herbs that interest me the most.

A few years ago I decided to put two passions together and make a series of herbal jellies. I chose cranberries as my base, because cranberries have a delicate flavour and a beautiful red colour. I started with mint. The marshes south of Gimli have plenty of wild mint, and a walk through marsh grasses will evoke the scent of the crushed mint. I took two cups of packed mint leaves and blanched them with hot water. I let them stand for about two hours, then drained them and added equal parts of cranberry juice to the mint infusion. I made jelly from this juice as I would have for cranberries alone. The result was a beautiful and bold-tasting cranberry mint jelly.

I branched out. I made rosemary-cranberry jelly, thyme-cranberry jelly, sage-cranberry jelly, and rose petal-cranberry jelly. Each was a complete success. I experimented using these jellies with different meals. The rosemary is particularly good with lamb, as is the mint, but they all seem to work well with whatever you cook. In Gimli you are in the middle of wonderful wild foods. All they require is a bit of work and a bit of imagination.

Beachcombing

All my life I have collected lucky stones. It may be that lucky stones are available everywhere from Timbuktu to Larnaca and places between, and the world may be full of collectors, but the only lucky stones I know or care about are on the shores of Lake Winnipeg. Let me explain. Lucky stones are flat limestone stones with a hole in the middle. The hole might be only a pinpoint so you have to hold the stone up to the light to see it, or it might be big enough to wear the stone as a ring. How the hole got there is a mystery, though it probably has to do with fossils and erosion.

Lucky stones are not easy to find. They are the same colour as the beach. Children learn to look for them, and they often make necklaces out of strings of lucky stones. Every house and every cottage along the lake has glasses full of lucky stones and beach glass collected by children (and often their parents).

In 2009 the ex-CBC broadcaster and cultural animateur

The Voyageur Guitar. Photo by Doug Nicholson, courtesy of Six String Nation.

Jowi Taylor began a project called the "Six String Nation." He took the idea of the popular shiny-steel National guitar and set out to produce a guitar that would incorporate elements of Canadian culture and landscape into an actual guitar, an actual "National" guitar. George Rizsanyi was charged with producing the guitar. (The guitar's nickname is Voyageur.)

The guitar incorporates such Canadian icons as a piece of Wayne Gretzky's hockey stick, Pierre Elliott Trudeau's canoe paddle, a piece of the deck of the *Bluenose*, and a ceiling joist from the St. Boniface Museum. Sixty-four pieces in all, from every province and territory, make up the guitar. And there on the seventh fret is a lucky stone from Gimli, proudly representing everything that Gimli stands for.

Here's how it got there. I got a phone call from my cousin Katrina, an artist and musician in Toronto, asking if I had any ideas for the guitar, anything that would stand for Manitoba.

"Sure," I said. "Gimli lucky stones."

A few days later Janet Stewart from the CBC arrived at the door of my cottage in Gimli.

"Tell me about lucky stones," she said.

I told her about Lake Agassiz and the limestone cliffs that inhabit the aquifer that remains under Manitoba, and the fossils that are everywhere. I showed her my collection of lucky stones and pointed out how hard they are to find. It was getting late and the sun was sinking.

"Do you mind if I look?" she asked. She was gone for perhaps fifteen minutes and came back with a dozen stones, about an all-time record.

A few days later I shipped off a beautiful lucky stone to Nova Scotia. A few weeks after that it was playing a concert in Winnipeg. And since then it has travelled all over Canada, helping to tell our story.

There are more objects than lucky stones on the Gimli beaches. The limestone fossils tell a prehistoric story, but there are more recent stories as well. Out at Willow Island, I found a spearhead thrown up onto the sand by a storm. The spearhead is made from amber and it has a flake of limestone attached to it. The chipping process that fashioned the spearhead is clearly visible. At some distant period, spruce gum dripped onto a limestone rock and dried as amber. And then some early ancestor chipped a flake from the rock and made a spear point.

But amber spearheads and arrowheads were not used by the first peoples from the Gimli area, I was told by a historian at the University of Manitoba. My specimen must have come from several hundred miles south. How it came to be here is a mystery, but it sits on my desk, demanding a story. Several weeks later I took some friends of mine on a picnic to the same spot. Their two little girls went searching for lucky stones and came back with a large amber scraping tool of a kind used for preparing hides and a perfect amber arrowhead.

Lake Winnipeg is large enough to have small tides, but it also develops wind tides of over four feet. The lake is shaped like an hourglass, large at the north end and funnelled through rocky narrows to the smaller south basin. When the wind is from the north, water pours from the north basin to the south, flooding fields and marshes. When the wind shifts to the south, water pours back into the north basin. In the ever-shifting swell of the lake, objects are picked up and delivered to new locations. Trees, logs, paddles, canoes, boats, life jackets, pop bottles, Styrofoam cups, shoes, diapers, hats, and docks find new homes. The lake shapes dead trees into driftwood that decorates homes all along the shore.

There are more rewards for the beachcomber than just the flotsam and jetsam of the lake. All through the enormous watershed of Lake Winnipeg, rivers and streams discover wonderful objects that they deliver to the lake. From the Rocky Mountains to the west, the north and south Saskatchewan rivers and the Assiniboine River deliver their bounty to the lake. The Red River brings us objects from the south and the Winnipeg River brings us treasure from the east. And every so often the Red floods, creating an enormous lake from Fargo to Winnipeg, swallowing whole farmyards and sending them for us to find and collect.

Not all the gifts that the lake delivers are equally welcome. In July fish flies descend on us, at times blotting out the sun. Anyone who has forgotten to turn off outside lights during fish fly season will know the horrors of their arrival.

Fish flies are born, mate, and die in about twenty-four hours. Adult fish flies do not have mouths and they do not eat.

Billions of fish flies spend most of their lives under water in the form of larvae. They make tiny burrows in the bottoms of lakes, where they spend about two years eating and preparing for their adult form. Then in July they emerge from the water in the form of sylphs and they join their fellows in a mating dance. Soon after they touch land, they moult, shucking their original skins and developing new ones. You can see the empty husks clinging to trees, leaves, and buildings. And the adults are everywhere.

When I was young, I spent a summer working for the

town of Gimli. Our main task was to shovel up truckloads of foul-smelling fish fly corpses from under street lights, neon lights, and the lights of stores and buildings. Fish fly season lasts for a couple of weeks as new hordes of flies are born and die. When female fish flies have mated, they fall into the water, where their eggs will begin the process of creating a new generation.

During the main mating season, fish flies can fall so thick on the streets that the roads are dangerously slippery. They can settle on cars so that they are four inches thick and they must be cleared before you can drive. They stain clothing and discolour car seats and windows. On the other hand, they are a rich source of food for birds and for the fish in the lake. A long fish fly season means a good fishing season. And the people who make their living from the lake welcome them.

Herbs of the Interlake

*A*rmoracia rusticana, better known as "horseradish," was named the herb of the year for 2011 by the International Herb Association. July is National Horseradish Month in the United States. Horseradish is one of the oldest culinary herbs and has been used for both cooking and medicinal purposes for nearly 4,000 years. It probably was first cultivated in southeastern Europe, and in particular in Ukraine. The Interlake area of Manitoba is blessed with plenty of Ukrainians and a good supply of horseradish. It grows wild, but is probably a garden escapee from Ukrainian and Polish farms in the area.

There are many sites where the plant grows wild by the side of the road. A few kilometres south of Gimli and just west of Highway 8, you can find a patch nearly a kilometre long with thousands of plants. The municipality regularly sprays the ditch in an attempt to control weeds, but the horseradish seems impervious to such assaults and comes back every year.

You can dig up plants or even just parts of plants and plant them in your own garden, but you should be aware that once they take root, they are nearly impossible to dislodge. I once planted some near my garage and tried to remove it a few years later. It had spread under the tarmac in my driveway and made its way right up through the asphalt. One of my brothers transplanted some into his garden, and when he finally sold his house, he sold the horseradish with it.

Horseradish is incredibly easy to prepare, but there are a few cautions. Use only the younger, smaller roots. Old roots can be tough and woody and relatively tasteless. Peel a couple of roots and cut into about a dozen pieces, each a couple of centimetres long. Pulse in a food processor until you get the consistency you want. Add white vinegar and salt to taste while processing. Seal in a glass jar and keep refrigerated. It will last for a month and a half. You can add heavy cream and dill if you want to make a sauce for beef. Horseradish is particularly pungent and can make your eyes water. Be sure to keep a window open when preparing it. You need only half as much homemade horseradish as a commercially prepared product.

Wild caraway (*Carum carvi*) grows throughout the Interlake, though I could not find any guide to herbs that mentions it. Still, the plant is identical to the photos of caraway that appear in books and the seeds (or fruits) that it produces are identical to those you can buy commercially. I first found it growing at Willow Island, but soon discovered that it is extremely common, growing on the sides of roads throughout the area. The plant grows low to the ground, about half a metre in height. It has feathery leaves and small white flowers. Caraway seeds are the main flavouring in rye bread and are also used to flavour cakes, breads, and cheeses. It is usually added to sauerkraut and cabbage soup. It is a highly invasive plant and is persistent and self-seeding, though it is a biennial.

In the areas around Gimli and Fraserwood, it ripens in early August, between the first and second week. The seeds are brittle and are hard to collect because they fall from the plant very easily. I have found that the best way to collect them is to find a patch with many plants, pick the whole plant, and put it into a green garbage bag. Then you can shake the bag to thresh the seeds, keeping the seeds that come free and discarding the stalks and leaves. You will probably find a quite a lot of chaff and a fair number of small spiders, but a careful winnowing will yield two or three handfuls of the precious seeds.

These can be used in any of the recipes in which you use commercially grown caraway seeds. But there is another special link between these seeds and local culture. The Icelandic national drink, Brennivin, often referred to as "black death," is flavoured with caraway. I have found that if you get some good quality (Icelandic) vodka, pour out one drink's worth and refill the bottle with about a tablespoon full of caraway seeds, then put the bottle in the freezer of your refrigerator, you will have a homemade version of Brennivin that is indistinguishable from the commercial variety. You will also have the satisfaction of making it from scratch, and you will pay less than you would have at the liquor store. Whether it is worth the effort is up to you to decide.

Gull on the beach.

Birds of the Interlake

There are moments when the world has a special luminosity. This has nothing to do with darkness and light, though that is another question. I was driving down the dike on the west side of the lagoon, looking over to my cottage and the narrow strip of lawn that separates us from the lake. Gulls were everywhere, and terns dived into the water. The air was filled with an almost reckless energy. A fox peered over the other side of the reeds towards the road I was driving on. I was prepared for the usual miracles of life and discovery, but I was not prepared for the exuberance and abundance I encountered. Sitting on the bank were several hundred golden plovers. My ancestors, the Icelanders, called them "loas," and they were always the sign of spring. This was late September and they should not have been here. But they were. Their black and gold plumage punctuated the autumn reeds and rushes. And in a moment, I was suddenly transformed. My life here in Canada was bonded with all my ancestors in Iceland.

Manitoba is one of the best places in the world for bird watching. Both the Mississippi Flyway and the great Central Flyway cross over parts of Manitoba, and birders looking to add to their life lists can easily find rare and exotic birds. Some species, unfortunately, are rare because their habitat is reduced, and farming practices have endangered birds through pesticides and fertilizers.

When I was a boy my family grew up on the edge of marshes and a lagoon on the west side of Lake Winnipeg. In the fall high waters would flood the marshes and reach across my mother's vegetable garden and right into our backyard. For weeks in September and October, the sky was black with migrating ducks and shorebirds. We lived with the sound of shotguns from early morning until dark, but there were so many birds that the hunters didn't seem to make any difference. The sound of the birds was a cacophony so loud that it interrupted ordinary conversation. Our gentle old dog, Bowfy, who could not ordinarily be enticed into the house with treats, came in and hid, trembling, under the bed.

I grew up in a family of hunters. All my uncles, brothers, and cousins hunted, and many of them still do. I remember a hunting culture that emphasized safety and respect for the birds and animals that we hunted. We did not hunt for fun. We hunted for food, though, as time went on, that became increasingly less of an argument for hunting. Hunting became more of an occasion for male bonding. In spite of that I became increasingly unable to kill things, and several years ago I gave it up entirely.

Still, I do remember certain joyful moments, though what I remember most is the sense of community. When I was fourteen my uncle Charley bought me my first shotgun. He had gone to Grand Forks for his honeymoon, and on the way back he stopped at Sears, Roebuck's and bought me a bolt-action twenty-gauge shotgun. It was clear to me even then that I had gone through a rite of passage that welcomed me to the male hunting culture. I was immensely grateful, even though the gun came with the rider that as I got older I was to pass the gun on to younger members of the family. And I did that.

What I remember most about those hunts is a sense of loneliness. Guns are dangerous, and the older members of our group sat the younger members in blinds or in boats alone so that we would not shoot each other or ourselves. We started early. First there was the boat ride out to the marshes. Then we were distributed around the hunting area to wait for the morning's first flight. I remember sitting on a muskrat house, a mound of rushes and reeds, watching a spider spin an intricate web. When the sun rose out of the lake, it lit up the drops of water on the web so that they formed a jewelled necklace. And as I studied the spider, a fast, small flock of teals flew right over my head.

In the fifties and sixties, ducks were everywhere, but we saw very few geese. Those who wanted to shoot geese had to drive west to Saskatchewan. Then, year by year, the fly-way for Canada geese and snow geese moved eastward until the ducks were replaced, and geese were so common they became a nuisance. Now, they are a traffic hazard and they congregate on urban lawns.

Though hunting was almost entirely a male practice, women played a part that they probably did not desire. The birds that the hunters harvested had to be plucked and cleaned, and that job fell to women and children. Long before I ever shot a bird, I had plucked and cleaned dozens. My mother, who had also grown up in a hunting family, pretended that she was keen to prepare the birds for cooking. First, she and whichever children could be forced into service plucked the birds. Then, Mother built a small fire and singed the birds to get rid of the difficult pinfeathers. Then, she cut a line between the bird's legs and pulled out all the insides, reserving the gizzard, heart, and liver. It was a hard and thankless job, and one of the reasons I quit hunting. A nearby Hutterite colony would do the work at very little expense, but the women who did the work did not seem to do it willingly, and I could not justify saving my mother from odious work by passing it on to the Hutterite women.

The men paid most of their attention to game birds, and though they could identify any duck in flight, they could not tell the difference between the many sparrows, warblers, and wrens that twittered and played at the edges of their vision. Mother, on the other hand, fed table scraps to the whisky jacks that lived in the bush every winter. Every summer she led us out into the front yard just at dusk to listen to the whip-poor-will. She tamed chickadees, and she taught us the names of the common birds: robins and crows and pigeons and sparrows. She had her favourites. She would empty the house by making everyone come out to see a mountain bluebird or a snowy owl.

One year not so long ago, she had a run-in with a deranged robin. It arrived at her bedroom window one morning and started pecking on the glass. It pecked all through the day and into the dark. The next morning it was there again, pecking at the glass and fouling the window with its excrement. It began to get on her nerves, but no one could suggest a remedy. My father chased it away, but it was almost always back in a few minutes. Finally, Father caught it in his hands and held it while I drove the car a full mile west, and we turned it out into a field of flax. It was back the next morning, as if pecking at the window were its full-time job. Mother would not let us kill it, and so it carried on through late July and into mid-August. Then, suddenly, it was gone. Mother suspected that it had been murdered, and I briefly fell under suspicion. I denied culpability, and the mystery remained for years until an uncle confessed to me, but not to Mother, that it was he who had ended its reign of terror. He claimed that he had done it only to save her sanity.

My mother, like many farm wives, decided to add to the family income by keeping chickens. My father, who liked to think big, built a twenty-metre-long chicken house at the end of a trail that led into the bush. He didn't consider that bags of grain and pails of water might need to be carried a long way to feed the chickens. The chicken house was equipped with a number of brooders, under which the baby chicks could huddle until they were big enough to make their way in the world. The day that one thousand chicks arrived, packed into large cardboard boxes, was a day of excitement. There were seven children in my family, and their squeals were as loud as the combined chirping of a thousand chicks. The chicks were little yellow puffballs on stick legs, and they were terminally cute.

Not as cute, however, as the chicks that first saw the light of day in our basement. Besides the hens, we kept several roosters. Mother gathered up the fertilized eggs and put them into the incubator, a piece of equipment that looked like an old-style glass-fronted bookcase. Each row held six eggs, and there were six rows of eggs. Mother had four incubators and so she could accommodate 144 eggs. The rows were heated and lit so that each egg could be seen. I remember sitting on a chair in the basement, watching for the eggs to hatch. Soon, one chick pecked its way out of its shell and the others followed in rapid succession. They were little wet things whose feathers clung to them as if they had arrived in water. A few minutes in the brooder and they were as yellow and fluffy as the commercial variety.

Chickens are amazingly intelligent, though modern methods of raising them in crowded conditions without any chance to exercise gives them very little chance to show their smarts. Our chicken house (we did not call it a "coop") was surrounded by a large yard fenced in with chicken wire. The birds were free-range chickens, though, again, we did not use that phrase. They dined on grain of various kinds, ate grasshoppers and insects, and were given crushed oyster shells to strengthen the shells of their eggs.

When my son, Vincent, was born, I decided that a proper father should be able to teach his children the names of birds, animals, and wildflowers. I set out to educate myself. I went out to a bookstore and bought field guides to birds, mammals, wildflowers, mushrooms, weeds, trees, shrubs, lichens, and grasses. For two years I spent every spare minute with binoculars and field guides, walking and driving through the natural landscape of Manitoba's Interlake. That education is still ongoing and it has shaped my life ever since.

The first thing I learned is that you can see only the things you can name. If you don't learn the names of things in the natural world, you can walk through fields and forest and see only green plants, nameless trees, small grey birds, and yellow and blue flowers. We all have the experience of seeing something like a particular car or coat and once we have noticed it, it is everywhere. It's the same with birds, plants, and trees. Once you have named them, they are everywhere.

In the Bible, Adam is charged with naming the creatures of the world. It is an important job, and the sheer plenitude of objects that must be named is an enormous task. But naming is only the first step. Adam gives objects their essence through the act of naming, but we are not at the beginning of the world. If we are to understand the world, we must understand the particularity of each object.

Birders keep life lists, the names of birds they have seen and identified. Audubon, the greatest of all birdwatchers, killed thousands of birds so that he could study them. Killing creatures so that you can study them is perhaps not the best road to knowledge.

Every spring the red-winged blackbirds return to mate in Manitoba. The males use their red wings to attract mates. Each male tries to stake out and defend a territory. When he has chosen his space, usually a marshy patch near a tree, a reed, or a telephone pole, he finds as many mates as he can and defends the nests of his mates, many mates if he is successful, none if he cannot compete. He warns off intruders with a cry that sounds like the opening of a rusty gate. The care of the eggs is mostly left to the females, but when the young leave the nest, the roles are reversed. The male must now teach the young to fly and to form flocks.

In early July you will see a few immature blackbirds being scolded into a small flock by a single male. The females, having done their duty, hang around for a while, but their job is over. You will see immature birds trying to land on twigs and reeds that will not support them. They will crash into your screen door and cling to it until the father bird chases them off. After a few days they will be joined by another small flock and another senior male. As the flocks merge some of the senior males drop out. This continues into October or November, the flock gathering more members as smaller flocks merge until flocks of several hundreds of birds make test flights and raid farmers' fields. However large the flock becomes, it is led by only a few senior males.

Oddly, they share the same piece of the marsh as the yellow-headed blackbirds, who live communally. The yellowheads arrive about two weeks earlier in the spring than the red-wings and they leave a couple of weeks sooner in the fall. They like to gather on the sand beaches in the south end of Lake Winnipeg. You can often see yellow-heads with red-wings and orioles collecting the night's harvest of insects. It is impossible to resist taking out your camera, no matter how often you have seen this sight.

I have several times visited a bird sanctuary at the Salton Sea in southern California. The sanctuary is divided into several small lakes intersected by roads, and it is filled with birds who summer in Manitoba. At one point two of these lakes are next to each other. One is filled with thousands of red-wings and the other with thousands of yellow-heads. So the snowbirds are not the only creatures fleeing the Canadian winter.

When I first began my study of the natural world, I spent hundreds of hours driving around, looking for likely spots to watch birds. I made some wonderful discoveries. On a beach at Crow Island I found a family of Semipalmated Plovers. A couple of yards away was a family of piping plovers. These small shorebirds are so much alike that it is hard to tell them apart except for the fact that piping plovers are the colour of dry sand and semipalmated plovers are the colour of wet sand. Seven or eight tiny birds ran back and forth together until a call from one or the other of the mother birds sent them scurrying back to their own flocks. Piping plovers are nearly extinct now, but a sign on the beach at Sandy Bar near Riverton warns you that you are at a nesting site for piping plovers. A couple of years ago a portion of prime beach near the dock at Gimli was fenced off to protect a nesting pair.

I've always had a soft spot for woodpeckers. Downy and hairy woodpeckers were common in the yard at home. They appear identical, except that the hairy woodpecker is considerably larger than its downy cousin. People who hang up a chunk of suet in their yard will soon be rewarded by one of the black-and-white-striped birds.

My first encounter with the larger woodpeckers came at a place near Camp Morton. I had parked my car and heard a bizarre call that resembled Woody Woodpecker's call in all those kids' cartoons. It took no time to locate him. He actually looked like Woody. I trained my binoculars on that pileated woodpecker and watched the chips of wood fly from his efforts. After a few minutes an even larger pileated arrived. It swooped down at the smaller bird and sent it flying. I had apparently chanced upon a mother woodpecker and her newly fledged offspring. The young bird chased the mother around the edge of the yard. She immediately left him and moved on to another tree. He kept following, apparently pleased to be able to make the chips fly but uncertain why he was doing it. The yard was full of older poplar trees, some of which had fallen and others that had such large holes drilled in them that they looked as if they were on the verge of falling. Pileated woodpeckers drill holes so that sap will run into the holes and the bird can come back later and eat the insects that have been caught in the sap.

That same trip showed me a family of red-headed woodpeckers. There were two adult birds and four immatures. That was my first sighting of either of those woodpeckers. I have seen them both many times since, but that first sighting stands out clearly in my memory.

We have a cottage now with a faithful pair of olive-sided flycatchers. They nest under the eaves and they return every year. They raise two families every summer and they spend most of their time catching flies for their offspring. Males and females share the feeding of the young. In their few moments off duty, they find high points where they can survey their dominion. Usually, they choose the handle of my wheelbarrow, which I park in the same spot every summer.

Birds figure in literature, in religion, in mythology, in folk tales, and in ordinary discourse. On rare occasions the birds of mythology escape the tales in which they reside and make an appearance in real life. Just such an occasion happened in Gimli a few years ago. In Icelandic mythology the chief god, Odin, is accompanied on his way to and from battle by the twin ravens, Huginn and Muninn, thought and memory. They ride on his shoulders as he surveys the slaughter of battle.

One spring, just as the snow was melting, two ravens built a nest in the steeple of the Unitarian church in Gimli. Since the church had just undergone a renovation and a new paint job, the maintenance committee decided to take down the nest and get rid of the ravens. That was easier said than done.

The moment the nest was gone, the ravens began to rebuild it. The church tried to remove it again in the fall, but by the next spring it was up again. After that they left the steeple to the mythic gods and the determined ravens. The nest is still there by public demand.

There are certain days in the summer when the updrafts create currents of air that are irresistible to gulls and terns and pelicans. When that happens hundreds of white birds appear in the sky, their wings widespread as they coast on the wind in wide circles. They glide upward until they are mere specks in the distance. Then they slip down to a height of about sixty metres, and begin their slow rise once more.

One summer I met a young man with binoculars who was sharing my view. I told him how wonderful it was to watch the sheer joy of the birds. He corrected me. Birds, he told me, do not play. They do nothing for the sheer joy of flight. He was a student at the University of Manitoba who was doing a master's degree on gull behaviour. The birds, he said, were looking for food. The rising wind currents let them get high enough to find minnows swimming near the surface of the lake.

I did not argue, though I had plenty of arguments in my arsenal. If they found minnows, why didn't they settle down and eat them? In my experience most of the gulls we were watching did not eat fish. They ate insects that had died on the beach or whose dead bodies floated on the waves. They ate garbage. The local garbage dump had Bonaparte's gulls by the thousands. By midsummer most of the Franklin's gulls had wandered off and were out on their own business. And there was the unanswered question of why they looked so happy if they were only searching for their next meal.

I've spent most of my life intently watching the natural world, and I cannot believe that birds and animals do not lead emotional lives. Increasingly, scientists are discovering that our assumption that animals and birds have very little conscious life is not sustainable. Anyone who has a dog knows that a dog can be sad, humiliated, angry, sorry, happy, anxious, or excited. It is quite capable of displaying all the emotions we can feel ourselves.

Back in February 1996, I was sitting in my studio at Willow Island. I had a pen in my hand so I jotted down exactly what I saw:

At 3:45 a redpoll crashed into the sliding glass door on the north side of the studio. It is not uncommon for them to do that, and they are rarely injured, but this case looked more serious. The bird lay on its stomach in the snow and didn't move at all for about two or three minutes. Then a female redpoll hopped over to the injured bird. She pecked at it a couple of times, then climbed on top, spreading her wings. She pecked at its head quite fiercely several times. It looked almost as if she were trying to mate with the passive bird, also a female.

When I approached the window, the active bird flew into a tree near the bird feeder, but only about a dozen feet away. It looked now as if the passive bird had moved its head a bit and opened its eyes, but I couldn't be sure. I watched for another three or four minutes, but the bird was motionless, and I thought it was likely dead. I put on my jacket to go out and see whether the bird was alive or dead, though I was quite certain it wasn't going to survive.

I took a towel from the bathroom, thinking I might wrap it up to keep it warm, but before I went outside, the active bird came back. It repeated the same action, tentatively pecking at the passive bird, then mounting it and performing some form of avian resuscitation.

Again, it pecked fiercely at the head, and this time, the passive bird suddenly flew off with the active bird. It was obviously still confused and it nearly hit the window again, but the two flew away and apparently the stunned bird survived.

This is only anecdotal evidence, I admit, but anecdotal evidence is evidence nevertheless. I believe in science and the scientific method, but we must be careful not to use such evidence to give pain to small creatures, who after all, can love us.

A Flight of Birds

I remember blue-winged teals in tight formation skimming over an October marsh, the sound of shotguns in the middle distance. I remember red-winged blackbirds filling the sky as they prepared for their southern journey. I remember fulmars hovering over an Icelandic river just where the fresh water meets the sea. But I am not interested in those birds of memory that take me back to events that have passed. I am more interested in the birds of imagination, the birds that provide segues between events in a narrative.

I was once hired to fix the narration for a film whose producers were unsatisfied with the script. I spent a long time hovering over a Steenbeck, a machine that allows you to cut film with a razor and patch it together with Scotch tape. I didn't actually do the cutting and pasting, but I had to time the narrative segments and replace them with my new words. The most difficult problem was to create a new narrative to fill the space between a drunken beach party and a service in a synagogue over a flight of gulls rising from a lake in only eleven seconds. I was looking for a voice that could make sense of images I had no part in constructing.

I was working with an old and inadequate technology, and I'm not sure whether my solution was any better than the original. But it raised for me the question of how to get from one place to another in a narrative or any other form of art: music, theatre, or dance. Of course, you can just stop and after a short pause begin again. That doesn't interest me, but the segue does: the connection that ties things together so that they both make sense.

There's a scene in the movie *Funny Face* where Audrey Hepburn wears a wedding dress, not to get married but to be photographed. Fred Astaire, who plays the photographer and Audrey's prospective lover, has taken her to a place near a church where swans swim in a tiny stream. Audrey has tears in her eyes because she is in love with Fred, but he doesn't seem aware of it. The screen goes momentarily to grey, and then a flock of white doves fills the screen and we are returned to the narrative. A perfect segue.

But that's not all. Later in the film we find her once again in the same wedding dress, at the same church with the same swans swimming in the same tiny stream. Again, she has tears in her eyes and again the screen fades to a flight of doves and she is returned to the narrative that is no longer the same narrative. The mise-en-scène, though identical in its production, is not identical to itself. The passage of time has given it a new meaning.

The film was released in 1957 and I saw it then. I was seventeen and in love with Audrey Hepburn. Fred Astaire was clearly too old for her, and that gave the film an oddly obscene flavour, that kind of tinge of old man's fantasy that inhabits Woody Allen's films. I watched the film again the other night because I wanted to see the flight of doves once more. They flew on schedule, and I found myself still in love with Audrey Hepburn, and I still didn't like Fred Astaire, though his dancing, which I had forgotten in the intervening years, was technically interesting but only as a foreshadowing of Michael Jackson in *Thriller*.

And I had nearly forgotten Audrey's eyes, dark eyes set in the face of a survivor, someone who had known hunger and fear but who could convey wonder, eyes like a flight of birds. Eyes like my mother's eyes.

The day my mother died Bohemian waxwings gathered by the hundreds in the trees that surrounded my father's house. I had driven out from the city to Gimli with my three sisters, and after gathering briefly with the rest of the family, we drove out to my studio to write her obituary. The studio is mostly glass overlooking the lake and a small bay. The bay is lined with ancient ash trees and willows. As soon as we arrived, the trees filled with waxwings slurring their rattling trill as they landed and took off. We worked for two hours, then headed back to town, accompanied by several flocks of birds.

A segue, I suppose, a transition from one kind of life to another, signalled by a flight of birds. And ever since, I have thought of waxwings as Mother's birds, and when I have seen them, prepared for change.

Reprise

Earlier in this book I referred to myself as "thrice ad-reams." I first encountered that phrase back in high school when we studied DH Lawrence's "Snake." Lawrence used the phrase to describe the slow, languid movement of the snake that he both desires and fears. Later, I found the expression "John a dreams" in Shakespeare's *Hamlet* in the scene in which Hamlet berates himself for his inaction when confronted with his father's death. The expression lingered in my mind as a synonym for daydreaming, but I never thought of it as a kind of lazy, mindless state. I imagined a more active state of deep thought and concern.

Both remembering and imagining are ways that the mind moves in time and space. We recreate the past through memory and we construct a future through our imagination. In Icelandic mythology the god Odin travels with two ravens, Huginn and Muninn, thought and memory.

The act of writing is a god-like act. We try to create

something new out of our thoughts and our memories. We do this best in a state of being "thrice adreams." This book has been an act of dreaming a life. This is not history. I make no claim for accuracy. But I have enjoyed remembering and imagining, and I hope you have too.

Acknowledgements

"Herbs of the Interlake," "The Ice Carnival, "The Stores of Gimli," "The Sporting Life," "Icelanders and Ukrainians," "The Best of All Possible Worlds," "Christmas in Gimli," and "Living on the Lake" were all published in the *Interlake Pulse* magazine in somewhat different versions than appear here. Portions of "Prelude" appeared in the *Interlake Pulse* under the name, "True Story." A portion of "Three Mothers" was originally published in the *Interlake Pulse* as "A Pioneer Woman." A portion of "A Fish Story" was published in the *Interlake Pulse* as "A Fishy Story." "First Arrivals," and "The Bright Lights of Winnipeg Beach," and "Berry Picking in Gimli" appeared as somewhat different versions in *H20 Magazine.* The final section of "First Arrivals" is from an essay titled "The Myth of Beginnings" first published in *Border Crossings.* "Summer Sports," appeared in a somewhat different form in *Islendingadagurinn*, the program for the Icelandic Celebration.

Many thanks to the team at Turnstone Press including Jamis Paulson and Sharon Caseburg, and especially to Sarah Ens for her excellent proofreading and editor Patricia Sanders to whom I am indebted. And of course Mhari Mackintosh whose patience allowed me to finish the book and to all the Interlake folk who appear in many guises.